Transportation Operations

I0415721

U.S. Marine Corps

PCN 143 000083 00

DEPARTMENT OF THE NAVY
Headquarters United States Marine Corps
Washington, D.C. 20380-1775

5 September 2001

FOREWORD

Marine Corps Warfighting Publication (MCWP) 4-11.3, *Transportation Operations*, addresses the fundamental principles required for the planning and execution of Marine air-ground task force (MAGTF) transportation operations. This manual provides an overview of transportation support and motor transport organizational structure, transportation task organizations, movement fundamentals, procedures, and capabilities.

MCWP 4-11.3 provides a broad doctrinal overview for commanders and their staffs on transportation support and motor transport tasks and functions in support of the MAGTF. Specifically, it gives general planning requirements, command relationships, support requirements and considerations, and capabilities.

MCWP 4-11.3 supersedes FMFM 4-9, *Motor Transport*, dated 27 April 1992 and FMFM 4-3, *MAGTF Landing Support Operations*, dated 25 January 1994.

Reviewed and approved this date.

BY DIRECTION OF THE COMMANDANT OF THE MARINE CORPS

/s/
EDWARD HANLON, JR.
Lieutenant General, U.S. Marine Corps
Commanding General
Marine Corps Combat Development Command

DISTRIBUTION: 143 000083 00

TRANSPORTATION OPERATIONS

TABLE OF CONTENTS

Chapter 3. Transportation Command and Control

Appendices

CHAPTER 1. TRANSPORTATION OVERVIEW

Sub-Functions

The sub-functions of transportation include—

- Motor Transport.
- Materials Handling.
- Landing Support.
- Embarkation.
- Freight/Passenger Transportation.
- Aerial Delivery.
- Port and Terminal Operations.

Motor Transport

Motor transport is surface transportation using wheeled vehicles. It is the most versatile mode of transport. It links the aerial ports, ocean ports, supply centers, rail, and inland waterway terminals. During combat operations, motor transport links combat service support (CSS) units and combat units. It is an all-weather mode of transport that the MAGTF commander can use over any trafficable terrain, to include off-road. Motor transport units can move nearly any type of cargo. They can provide local, line or zonal hauls. The commander may use organic, attached, contracted or supporting motor transport assets to support operations.

The Marine Corps motor transport system provides an effective means of meeting the requirements of the landing force for ground transportation. The tactical motor transport fleet is specifically designed to provide ground mobility to combat, combat support, and CSS units. The restructured CSS organization has resulted in a change in motor transport operations philosophy, a reorganization of motor transport units, and a reallocation of associated resources within the Marine Corps.

Function

The function of motor transport is to provide elements of the MAGTF with tactical and logistical motor transport support. This support includes the transportation of personnel, weapons, communications equipment, general cargo, specialized cargo, and shelters/containers conforming to American National Standards Institute/International Standardization Organization (ISO) specifications.

Capabilities

Marine Corps motor transport units are organized and equipped to perform missions under all environmental conditions. Only minor changes in equipment are required for extreme conditions of climate and terrain. In most cases, these changes are made by the installation of special kits. Motor transport equipment includes vehicles that are designed to meet all assigned motor transport missions. Increased efficiency of authorized motor transport assets is achieved through—

- Equipment standardization with fewer types of vehicles.
- Centralized control of vehicles assigned combat service support missions to ensure effective, on time delivery of support.
- Decentralized control of vehicles providing tactical mobility missions to combat units to ensure maximum flexibility.

Materials Handling

Materials handling is the movement of materials to, through, and from productive processes; in warehouses and storage; and in receiving and shipping areas. (Joint Publication [JP] 1-02, *Department of Defense Dictionary of Military and Associated Terms*) Materials handling equipment (MHE) is a group of mechanical devices for handling of supplies with greater ease and economy. (JP 1-02) Effective use of available MHE is essential to movement control and maintaining the throughput of supplies and equipment.

Landing Support

Landing support is the assistance provided to effect the efficient and responsive throughput of personnel, supplies, and equipment during the ship-to-shore movement phase of the amphibious assault or across beaches in support of operations ashore. It includes control of the flow of personnel and material across the beach and into landing zones. Landing support does not end when the MAGTF completes the assault. It continues through landing of the assault follow-on echelons (AFOEs). Landing support also includes the evacuation of casualties and enemy prisoners of war (EPWs) during the early stages of the assault.

Embarkation

Embarkation is the process of putting personnel and/or vehicles and their associated stores and equipment into ships and/or aircraft. (JP 1-02) A characteristic of successful operations is the rapid and effective manner in which a MAGTF can establish itself ashore. The MAGTF must expand its power and size to the maximum in the shortest possible time. This requires a rapid and orderly buildup of personnel and material. The ability to do this depends largely on the manner in which the MAGTF has loaded its transportation vessels/assets for deployment. Proper loading increases the flexibility of the MAGTF.

Freight/Passenger Transportation

Freight/passenger transportation includes the procurement of both Department of Defense (DOD) and commercial transportation assets. It encompasses the movement of personnel, equipment, and supplies via all modes of transportation (air, bus/truck, rail, and water). It includes planning for troop movements on scheduled or chartered trains, aircraft, and buses in continental United States (CONUS) and overseas. It also entails port calling of passengers for overseas movement.

Aerial Delivery

Aerial delivery is the in-flight delivery of specially rigged equipment and supplies to land-based forces. It is performed by either fixed-winged or rotary-winged aircraft from varying altitudes.

Port and Terminal Operations

A port is a place at which ships may discharge or receive their cargoes. It includes any port accessible to ships on the seacoast, navigable rivers or inland waterways. (JP 1-02) A port operation is the expeditious loading and unloading of personnel, supplies, and equipment.

Terminal operations are defined as the reception, processing, and staging of passengers; the receipt, transit storage, and marshaling of cargo; the loading and unloading of ships or aircraft; and the manifesting and forwarding of cargo and passengers to destination. (JP 1-02)

Whereas port operations are specific to the loading and unloading of ships, terminal operations encompass any or all modes of transportation (air, rail, water, land, pipeline) and throughput procedures. A terminal can be any military or commercial transportation facility.

Throughput Concept

Throughput is the flow of sustainability assets in support of military operations, at all levels of war, from point of origin to point of use. It involves the movement of personnel and material over lines of communications (LOCs) using pipelines and distribution systems. (JP 1-02)

For the purposes of this publication, the throughput concept is defined as the logistical infrastructure that links—

- Production logistics to consumer logistics.
- Sources of operating forces' military capability to the sustainability of those forces.

The throughput system is composed of LOCs; the pipeline and associated distribution systems; posts, bases, and airfields; and civilian agencies and supporting forces, which operate those facilities and installations.

The throughput concept involves all those pipeline-oriented functions, activities, facilities, procedures, and control methods necessary to create, maintain, and sustain the force. In relation to the functions of operational logistics and CSS, such functions and activities are primarily transportation and supply related. However, throughput ranges from contracting for the initial movement from points of origin to points of departure, to in-transit support, to ship-to-shore movement, to the inland transfer of personnel, supplies and equipment to points of use.

Deployment Transportation

Concept of Deployment Support

Deployment and redeployment of forces and support of those forces are functions of command. The deploying MAGTF/unit is the supported command. Units and organizations that support the deploying MAGTF/unit are supporting commands.

Deployment support is support provided to forces to allow the efficient and effective movement of forces from the point or origin to port of embarkation (POE), POE to port of debarkation (POD), and POD to final destination. Deployment support allows the deploying MAGTF/unit to properly marshal, stage, embark, debark, and employ.

Supporting commands provide support to deploying MAGTFs during deployments and ensure that forces, sustainment, replacements, and supplies are available, prepared, and moved to the POE in the types and amounts required by the deploying MAGTF. This is accomplished by activating control organizations, reserve units and base/station support organizations, and by coordinating with the supporting establishment, Headquarters Marine Corps, and the transportation component commands of United States Transportation Command (USTRANSCOM).

Deployment planning encompasses both deliberate and crisis action planning.

Deployment execution can encompass several phases, including—

- Preparation for movement.
- Movement from unit areas to marshaling areas.
- Movement from marshaling areas to staging areas at air and/or sea ports of embarkation (A/SPOE).
- Movement from A/SPOE to air and/or sea ports of debarkation (A/SPOD).
- Movement from A/SPOD to tactical assembly areas.

Deployment Agencies

MAGTFs deploy from permanent installations for training exercises, forward deployments, and combat operations. Regardless of the type of deploying force, designated transportation operating agencies control and coordinate the marshaling, embarkation, and movement of forces.

External

External organizations involved in transportation planning/execution may include—

- Supported commander in chief (CINC).
- Supporting CINC(s).
- Subordinate Joint Forces/Commanders such as Joint Task Forces (JTFs), Joint Logistics Over the Shore (JLOTS) Commander and Joint Interagency Task Forces (JIATFs).
- Other service components (U.S. Army, Navy, and Air Force) such as Army echelon above corps units.
- Fleet commander.
- USTRANSCOM and its subordinate commands:
  - Military Sealift Command (MSC).
  - Air Mobility Command (AMC).
  - Military Traffic Management Command (MTMC).
- Defense Logistics Agency (DLA).

Internal

Marine Corps commands may include—

- Headquarters, U.S. Marine Corps.
- Marine Force(s).
- Deploying Marine expeditionary forces (MEFs).
- Deploying MAGTF command element (if other than a MEF).
- Divisions, aircraft wings, and force service support groups (FSSGs) that are providing elements to the MAGTF.

- Bases and air stations from which the forces deploy.
- Marine Corps Materiel Command.

Deployment Modes

Transportation modes vary depending on the type of MAGTF, the purpose and duration of the deployment, and the anticipated employment. Deployments of MEFs generally require use of all transportation modes. MEFs are the most complex deployments from a transportation perspective, as elements of the MEF commonly deploy from different bases and stations, which may be in widely separated geographic areas.

Employment Transportation

Transportation within the AOR/Theater

Transportation in the area of responsibility (AOR)/ theater includes the organic assets of the MAGTF. It may also include transportation belonging to the joint force commander (JFC), coalition forces or the host

nation. Assets may include airlift, rail, trucks, ships, barges, and pipelines.

Movement Control in the AO

The component commander is responsible for movement control in the assigned area of operations (AO) and normally delegates this responsibility to subordinate commanders within whose zones of action or areas the movement takes place.

Movement Control in Theater Areas

When operating as part of a unified command or JTF, the MAGTF commander follows the traffic management and movement control regulations of that command. Normally, the higher commander establishes a movement control agency such as a joint movement center (JMC) to provide movement management services and highway traffic regulation. This agency coordinates with allied and host nation movement control agencies.

CHAPTER 2. TRANSPORTATION ORGANIZATIONS

Force Service Support Group

In addition to the motor transport assets of Transportation Support Battalion (TSB), most units within the FSSG are authorized motor transport equipment to meet organic lift requirements.

Note: The organizations described within this chapter are notional. Geographic location and unique or specific mission requirements may dictate that structure will differ from that depicted.

Transportation Support Battalion

The TSB provides motor transport and landing support for the MAGTF (see figure 2-1). The TSB can provide the nucleus of personnel and equipment from which a landing force support party (LFSP) or combat service support element (CSSE) is task- organized. The TSB has the assets required to support all types of Navy and Marine Corps operations.

Mission

Provide tactical throughput support and associated command and control (C2) for the MAGTF to facilitate the distribution of personnel, equipment, and supplies by air, ground, and sea.

Tasks

- Provide centralized command, control, and communications for landing support, distribution and throughput functions (including port and terminal operations), materials handling, air delivery support, convoy operations, and motor transportation during operations conducted by the MAGTF.

- Provide selected heavy equipment lift augmentation in support of the MAGTF.

- Transport personnel, equipment, and supplies within organic lift capabilities.

- Provide throughput and distribution of bulk, liquid, containerized, and dry cargo.

- Provide port and terminal operations at ports, beaches, airheads, railheads, and cargo terminals, and management of freight/passenger and breakbulk/container cargo throughput.

- Provide air delivery support for MAGTF operations.

- Perform basic engineer tasks required for landing support operations to include austere site preparations, construction/removal of obstacles and barriers, and establishment of routes of egress from the beach when properly augmented.

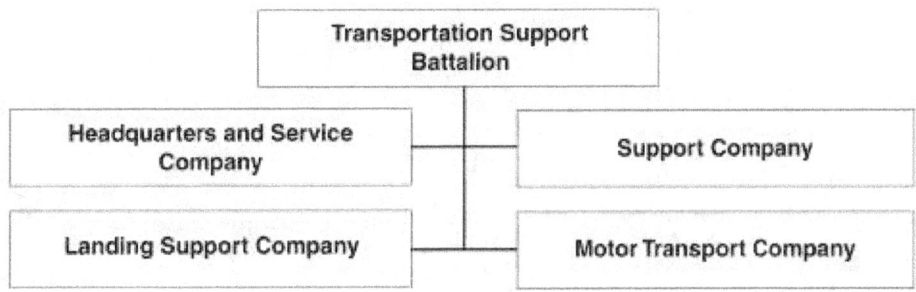

Figure 2-1. Transportation Support Battalion.

- Provide a nucleus for the task organization of LFSP/arrival and assembly operations group (AAOG) from organic assets to provide C2 structure for the landing support and distribution for initial CSS for MAGTF operations.

- Provide security for organic units.

Concept of Organization

The battalion is organized to plan, coordinate, and supervise the throughput and distribution functions in support of MAGTF operations. It is structured to facilitate task organization for operations conducted by the battalion in support of the MAGTF.

Concept of Employment

The battalion is structured to facilitate task organization for landing support and throughput operations conducted in support of the MAGTF. It is equipped to provide medium through heavy cargo transportation to the MAGTF. Additionally, the battalion provides the initial source for centralized CSS for MAGTF operations.

Headquarters and Service Company

Mission

Provide C2, administration, and command support functions for TSB, FSSG.

Tasks

- Provide command support functions to include supply, ordnance, information management, and food service support for the battalion.

- Provide organizational maintenance for ordnance and communication-electronic equipment.

- Provide support for the battalion's local security.

Concept of Organization

The company is organized to plan, coordinate, and supervise the command support functions for the battalion. It is structured to facilitate task organization for operations conducted by the battalion in support of MAGTF operations.

Concept of Employment

The company provides the command support functions to plan, coordinate, and supervise the general intermodal transportation, landing support, and throughput functions conducted by the battalion in support of the MAGTF.

Support Company

Mission

Provide MHE, container handling support, and organizational maintenance support for engineer and motor transport assets of the battalion in support of MAGTF operations (see figure 2-2).

Tasks

- Provide MHE support for the MAGTF beyond the organic capability of supported units.

- Provide specialized MHE and container handling support for the management of container/cargo throughput operations on beaches, at ports, railheads, airheads, and cargo terminals.

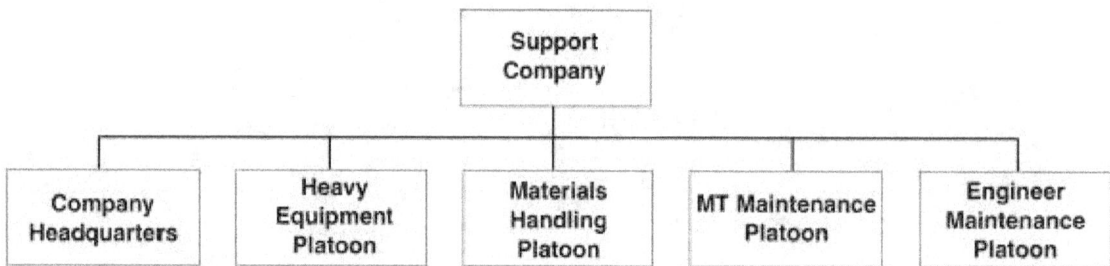

Figure 2-2. Support Company.

● Provide organizational (1st, 2d echelon) maintenance support for engineer and motor transport equipment organic to the battalion.

Concept of Organization

The company is organized to plan, coordinate, and supervise the command support functions of the company. It is structured to facilitate task organization for throughput operations conducted by the battalion in support of the MAGTF.

Concept of Employment

The company provides centralized support to expedite throughput operations. It is equipped with tactical engineering cranes, buckets, graders, forklifts, and light sets to facilitate operations. The company can be task-organized to provide CSSEs.

Landing Support Company

Mission

Provide direct support for landing and throughput operations at helicopter landing zones (HLZs), assault beaches, and airfields (see figure 2-3).

Tasks

● Provide shore party and/or helicopter support teams (HSTs) in direct support of assault and sustained operations.

● Prepare, mark, and control assault landing beaches or zones as required.

● Establish multi-class supply storage sites ashore.

● Coordinate the unloading of supplies and equipment from landing craft, ships, and helicopters through designated assault beaches and HLZs.

● Coordinate transportation support for the evacuation of casualties, noncombatants, and EPWs.

● Provide departure airfield control group/arrival airfield control group (DACG/AACG) to control and coordinate the loading and unloading of units deploying or redeploying by fixed-wing aircraft.

Concept of Organization

The company is organized to provide the nucleus of personnel and equipment required for a shore party group or AAOG.

Concept of Employment

The company provides direct landing support in support of amphibious and helicopterborne operations. When reinforced with battalion assets, it provides the nucleus for the shore party group and AAOG which provides initial throughput and sustainment for the MAGTF. Upon establishment of the CSSE, operational control passes to the CSSE commander for the continuation of direct landing support as required. The company coordinates local security for a colored beach. The company can provide AACG/DACG to support deploying/redeploying units.

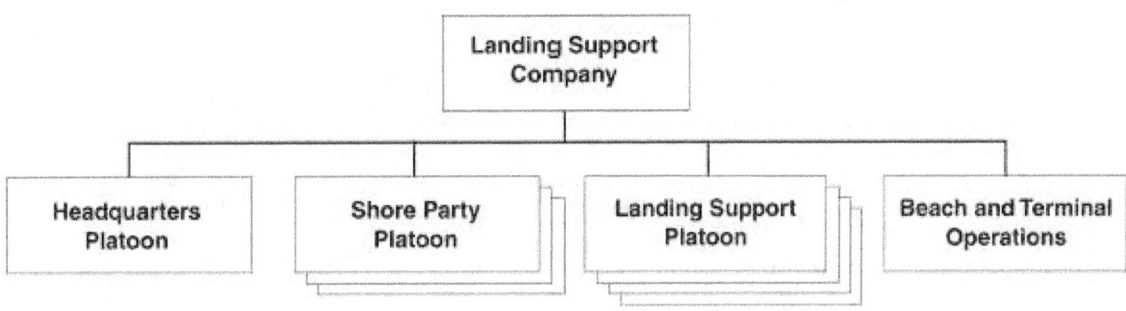

Figure 2-3. Landing Support Company.

Beach and Terminal Operations

Mission

Provide general transportation support to coordinate throughput operations for the MAGTF (see figure 2-4).

Tasks

- Provide personnel and equipment for the loading, unloading, and movement of supplies and equipment at ports, beaches, railheads, airheads, cargo terminals, dumps, and depots.

- Provide air delivery support.

Concept of Organization

Beach and terminal operations is organized to support throughput operations. It provides management and operation of ports, airheads, railheads, and other cargo/passenger terminal operations including aerial delivery support.

Concept of Employment

When directed, beach and terminal operations assumes responsibility for the throughput operations after control of beaches, ports, and terminals is passed to the CSSE. It provides aerial delivery support and, when augmented by other elements of the CSSE, controls air terminals to include conducting DACG/AACG operations.

Motor Transport Company, General Support

Mission

Provide general support, medium and heavy lift transportation support for throughput, and sustainment operations (see figure 2-5).

Tasks

- Provide distribution of bulk water (Class I) and bulk fuel (Class III and III[A]).

- Provide medium and heavy lift motor transport for the movement of bulk dry cargo, Class V and V(A), and heavy equipment.

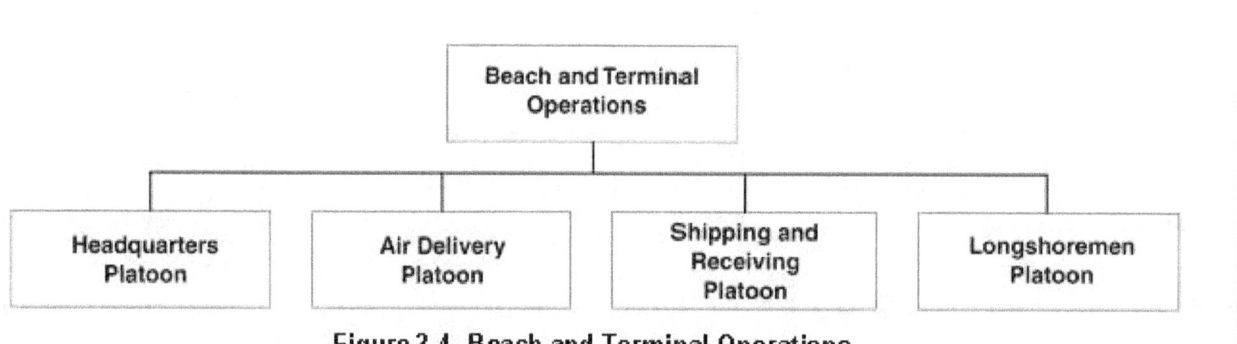

Figure 2-4. Beach and Terminal Operations.

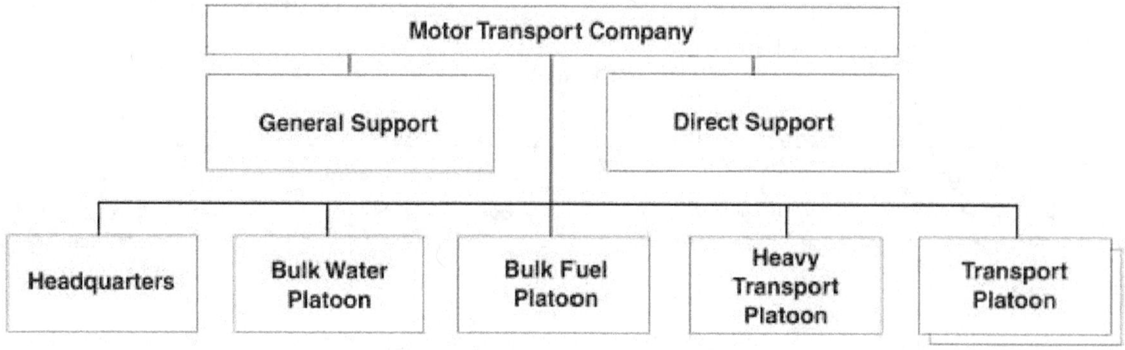

Figure 2-5. General Support.

- Provide unit and supply point distribution of bulk water and fuel.
- Augment the motor transport and supply distribution capabilities of the Direct Support Motor Transport Company, TSB, FSSG, as required.

Concept of Organization

The company is organized to plan, coordinate, and supervise the command, supply, and transportation support functions for the company. It is structured to facilitate task organization for operations conducted by the battalion.

Concept of Employment

The company provides medium and heavy lift motor transport and bulk fuel and water distribution. It is employed in general support to transport cargo, equipment, and personnel over extended distances for sustained periods of time. Organic equipment includes 5-ton tactical cargo trucks, Logistics Vehicle Systems (LVSs), and 40- and 70-ton semitrailers.

Motor Transport Company, Direct Support

Mission

Provide direct and general support, medium and heavy lift transportation support for throughput and sustainment operations of the CSSE in support of the MAGTF (see figure 2-6).

Tasks

- Provide line haul and distribution of bulk water (Class I) and bulk fuel (Class III and III[A]) for the CSSE.
- Provide medium and heavy lift motor transport for the movement of bulk dry cargo, Class V and V(A), and heavy equipment.
- Augment the personnel lift capability, as required, of elements of the MAGTF.

Concept of Organization

The company is organized to plan, coordinate, and supervise the command, supply, and transportation support functions for the company. It is equipped with 5- and 7-ton tactical cargo trucks, LVSs, and sixcon fuel and water modules.

Concept of Employment

The company is structured to provide sustained, direct support transportation to the CSSE, and general support transportation to the MAGTF. It transports cargo, equipment, fuel, water, and personnel over extended distances for sustained periods of time.

Marine Division Motor Transport

Subordinate elements of the division have motor transport equipment authorized for organizational use. Because of the limited quantities and specialized roles

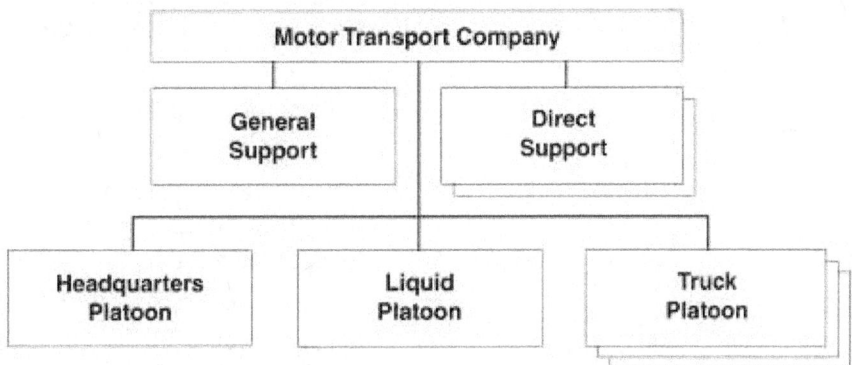

Figure 2-6. Direct Support.

of that equipment, it will normally not be available for routine logistical support.

Truck Company, Headquarters Battalion, Marine Division

The truck company provides limited tactical mobility to the Marine division. The company consists of a headquarters and three truck platoons containing two truck sections each (see figure 2-7). The company commander directs and controls all matters pertaining to company administration and support. The company headquarters supports the company commander in exercising C2 of the operating elements in the three truck platoons. The truck company is under the administrative control (ADCON) of the headquarters battalion commander. Operational tasking of the truck company is coordinated by the division motor transport officer. He makes recommendations as appropriate to the commander, usually via the principal staff officers, as requirements are developed.

The truck company is a combat support asset of the Marine division. It is capable of transporting the assault elements of two infantry battalions simultaneously. Truck platoons will normally be attached to or placed in direct support of infantry regiments and are capable of sustained operations on a 24-hour basis. Normally the tactical situation will require that motor transport assets of the truck company be used to augment the limited organic capability of subordinate division units.

The truck company is capable of providing organizational (1st and 2d echelon) maintenance for all organic equipment except communication equipment. Both 2d and 3d echelon maintenance for organic communication equipment are provided by communications company, headquarters battalion, division. Intermediate (3d and 4th echelon) maintenance for all other equipment is provided by maintenance battalion, FSSG. Selected items of equipment are listed in table 2-1.

Table 2-1. Truck Company, Selected Items of Equipment.

TAMCN	Description	Model	Qty
D0860	Trailer, Cargo, 1½-ton	M105A2	57
D0880	Trailer, Tank, Water, 400 Gallon	M149A1	13
D1059	Truck, Cargo 5-ton	M923	100
D1158	Truck, Utility, 1¼-ton	M998	12
D1212	Truck, Wrecker	M936	3

Motor Transport Section, Division Headquarters

The motor transport section, division headquarters, consists of the division motor transport officer and a small administrative staff. The motor transport officer performs the general duties of a special staff officer under the cognizance of the assistant chief of staff, G-4. The staff responsibilities of the division motor transport officer include—

- Supervising the planning and technical training and motor transport related duties and programs within the division.

- Coordinating planning for motor transport intelligence and the dissemination thereof.

- Conducting comprehensive analyses of all motor transport tasks required to implement the commander's plan.

- Maintaining liaison with higher, lower, and adjacent commands pertaining to motor transport matters.

- Analyzing and evaluating motor transport capabilities throughout the command.

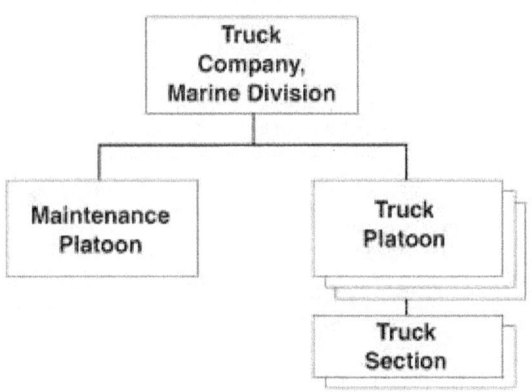

Figure 2-7. Truck Company, Marine Division.

- Coordinating all motor transport support requirements and directing commitments, as appropriate, to organizations best capable of providing the support required.

- Monitoring and providing technical supervision to all motor transport requirements, commitments, and movements of truck company.

- Supervising and coordinating the maintenance of required motor transport records and reports.

- Developing, coordinating, implementing, and monitoring command technical inspections for motor transport.

- Monitoring motor transport combat readiness in all subordinate organizations of the command.

- Advising the commander of all technical matters concerning motor transport.

Marine Aircraft Wing Motor Transport

Some subordinate elements of the Marine aircraft wing (MAW) have limited, special purpose motor transport equipment authorized for organizational use. Other than limited general purpose motor transport equipment, units of the MAW receive organic motor transport support from the Marine wing support squadrons (MWSSs).

Marine Wing Support Squadron, Marine Wing Support Group, MAW

Organic motor transport support for the MAW is provided by the MWSSs of the Marine wing support group (MWSG). There are four MWSSs in each MWSG. Each MAW has two MWSSs designed to support a fixed-wing (FW) aircraft group and two MWSSs to support a rotary-wing (RW) aircraft group. These are designated MWSS/FW and MWSS/RW, respectively. The exception to this is in 1st MAW, which has one FW and one RW MWSS.

The MWSS is organized to provide essential aviation ground support to the FW or RW components of an aviation combat element (ACE). An MWSS may also supplement the garrison support provided by a permanent Marine Corps air station. In addition to motor transport, this support includes explosive ordnance disposal, security and law enforcement, photographic services, air freight services, weather services, internal airfield communications, crash/fire/rescue and structural firefighting services, essential engineer services, expeditionary airfield services, aircraft and ground equipment refueling, aircraft recovery, messing facilities, medical services, training support, and internal nuclear, biological, and chemical (NBC) defense.

Motor Transport Operations Division

The motor transport operations division of the MWSS is organized into two branches: the light/medium motor vehicle branch and the heavy motor vehicle branch (see figure 2-8). Table 2-2, on page 2-8, presents a list of selected items of equipment.

The motor transport section, MAW consists of the wing MAW motor transport officer and a small administrative staff. The motor transport officer performs the general duties of a special staff officer parallel to those of the division motor transport officer.

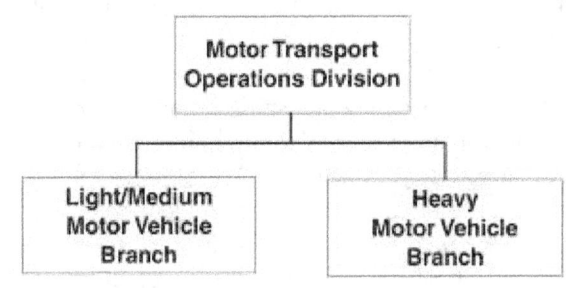

Figure 2-8. Motor Transport Operations Division.

Table 2-2. Truck Company, Selected Items of Equipment.

TAMCN	Description	Model	Qty
D0860	Trailer, Cargo, 1 1/2 ton	M105A2	57
D0880	Trailer, Tank, Water, 400 gal	M149A1	13
D1059	Truck, Cargo 5-ton	M923	100
D1158	Truck, Utility, 1 1/4-ton	M998	12
D1212	Truck, Wrecker	M936	3

Transportation Task Organizations LFSP

Fundamentals

The TSB is responsible for the MAGTF's landing support services and provides the units required to form the LFSP. The LFSP's mission is to perform specified combat service support operations for the landing force during the amphibious assault. It also provides initial landing support and combat service support to the landing force during the amphibious operation. The LFSP facilitates the MAGTF's ship-to-shore movement by—

- Supporting the landing plan.
- Avoiding excessive concentration of equipment, people, and supplies.
- Providing a uniform flow ashore of material required by the landing force.

The LFSP is peculiar to an amphibious operation. It is a temporary task organization composed of Navy and Marine Corps elements tasked to provide initial combat service support during the ship-to-shore movement. The LFSP's strength and composition are determined during the amphibious operation's initial planning phase. The LFSP may include units or detachments from the ground combat element (GCE), ACE, CSSE, and the Navy. The MAGTF's organization and mission, the number of landing beaches/zones through which the MAGTF will land, and the mission and size of the units assigned to the beaches/zones determine the LFSP's configuration. The LFSP is under the operational control (OPCON) of the commander, landing force (CLF) (see figure 2-9).

The LFSP provides CSS to the landing force until the CSSE is ashore and capable of assuming responsibility for logistics support. While the LFSP

organization may vary, it typically consists of a headquarters, two or more shore party groups and HSTs, a beach party group, and various special attachments (see figure 2-10).

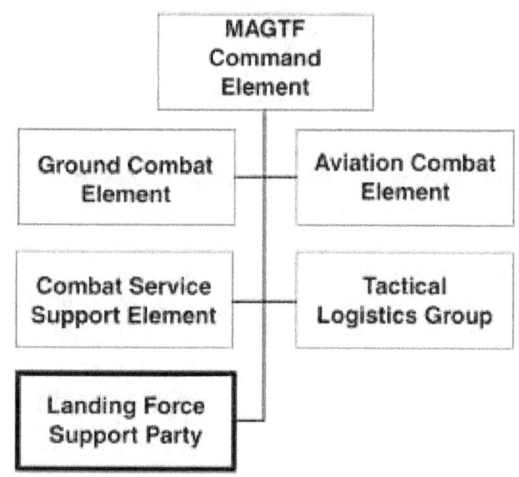

Figure 2-9. LFSP Relationship within the MAGTF.

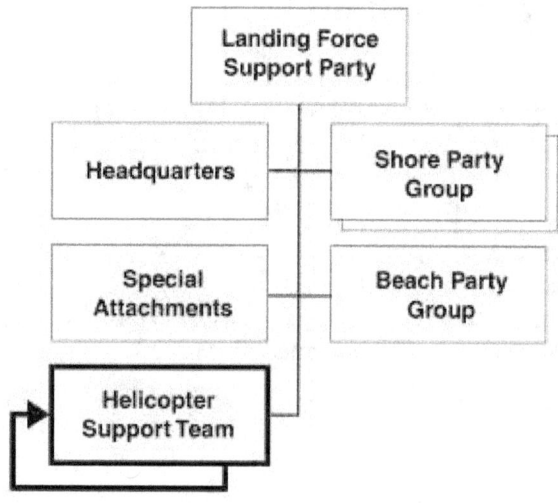

Figure 2-10. Basic Organization of the LFSP.

Headquarters

The LFSP headquarters controls and supervises landing support operations within the landing area as set forth in the landing force operation plan. The LFSP headquarters ensures effective landing support through close coordination, timely reinforcement, and consolidation of shore party group and beach party group activities.

During the initial stages of ship-to-shore movement, the LFSP headquarters typically remains afloat where it can best control and supervise the landing forces' landing support operations. However, operational necessity may require the LFSP headquarters to move ashore earlier. As more functions and capabilities move ashore, the LFSP headquarters grows accordingly. Once the CSSE, ACE, and naval beach group (NBG) are established ashore, they assume responsibility for their appropriate tasks.

Command and Administrative Section

TSB headquarters or the MAGTF CSSE provides the personnel needed to form the command and administrative section.

Medical Section

Medical battalion, FSSG provides the nucleus of the medical section. The medical section plans the LFSP's medical evacuation functions, supervises patient operations within the shore party and the HST's evacuation sections, and prepares medical reports.

Military Police Section

Normally, the military police (MP) section consists of personnel taken from the MP company, FSSG. This section supervises the shore party and HST's MP sections. In addition, this section establishes the landing force's EPW stockade and organizes and evacuates EPWs from the objective area.

Communications Section

The nucleus of the communications section is provided by the TSB or MAGTF CSSE and may be augmented from other sources. This section provides required communications ashore. Marine Corps Warfighting Publication (MCWP) 6-22, *Communications and Information Systems*, contains additional information on landing support communications.

The Motor Transport and Equipment Section

The TSB or MAGTF CSSE provides motor transport and equipment section personnel. Only those vehicles required by the LFSP headquarters operate under the direct control of this section. The remaining assets are assigned to augment the LFSP and are normally attached to the shore party team, shore party group, and HSTs.

Liaison Section

The liaison section consists of liaison personnel from units that are attached to or under the OPCON of the LFSP.

Shore Party Group

The shore party group provides landing support across the beach by assisting movement of troops and supplies, evacuating casualties and EPWs, and controlling landing craft and amphibious vehicles. Marine components of the shore party group perform tasks inland from the water's edge, and Navy components perform tasks seaward from the water's edge. The shore party group is capable of providing CSS to a regimental landing team over a designated (colored) beach. All tasks are performed under the direction of the shore party group commander, who is designated by the LFSP commander.

The shore party team lands ahead of the shore party group to assist with the initial landing. Once the shore party group moves ashore, shore party teams are absorbed into the shore party group. Shore party teams are capable of supporting a battalion landing team over a numbered beach.

The shore party group has a headquarters, two or more shore party teams, and special attachments as required (see figure 2-11, on page 2-10). The nucleus of the shore party group is drawn from the landing support company, TSB.

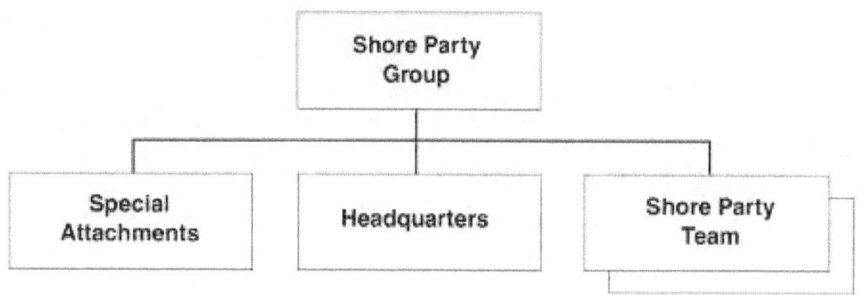

Figure 2-11. Shore Party Group.

Headquarters

The headquarters section controls and supervises landing support operations within the landing area as set forth in the landing force operation plan. It coordinates with the LFSP aboard ship, the tactical logistical group (TACLOG), and the landing force (see figure 2-12).

Command Section. The nucleus of the command section is drawn from the landing support company's headquarters. This section handles the shore party group's administrative functions.

Military Police Section. The MP section consists of the section leader of the attached MP unit and the assigned administrative and communications personnel. This section coordinates each of the shore party teams' MP operations and is absorbed by the CSSE once the shore party group dissolves.

Evacuation Section. When the evacuation section is established ashore, it assumes control of the shore party teams' evacuation sections. This section is comprised of personnel from the CSSE's attached medical units and assets from the ACE's helicopter units. This section maintains the records of evacuated personnel and evaluates the casualty evacuation procedures for effectiveness.

Communications Section. The communications section provides communications for the shore party

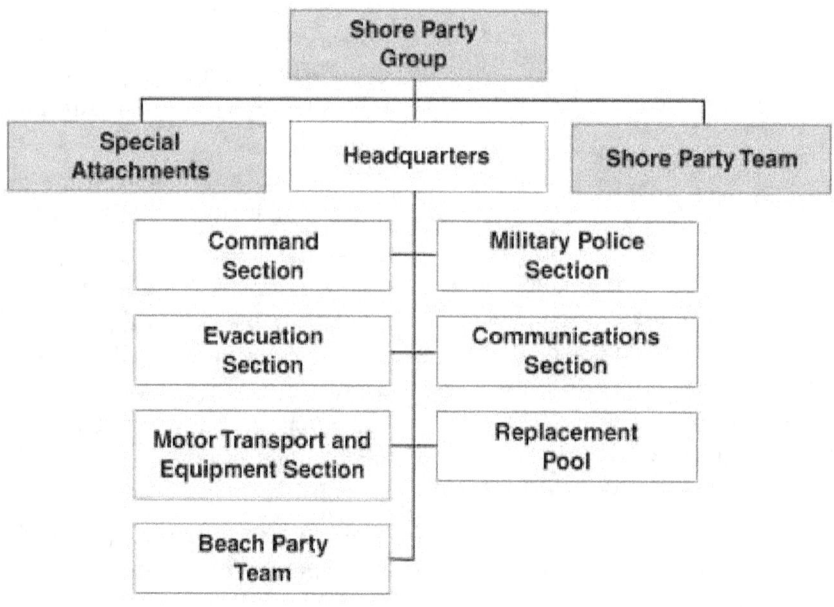

Figure 2-12. Headquarters, Shore Party Group.

group headquarters. Personnel and assets for this section come from the CSSE. Once the shore party group is established ashore, it coordinates communications established by the shore party teams and assumes control of the shore party team's communications section.

Motor Transport and Equipment Section. Once the shore party group assumes control of shore party team operations, this section assumes control of all motor transport functions and equipment attached to shore party teams. Personnel and assets for this section come primarily from the TSB.

Replacement Pool. The replacement pool consists of personnel waiting to be drafted into operation and are referred to as replacement units. Replacement units may be used to form ships platoon. Typically, replacement units assist the shore party in the accomplishment of general tasks. During the selective and general unloading phases, replacement units are used as longshoremen at unloading points and dumps in the beach support area (BSA).

Beach Party Team. See paragraph entitled "Beach Party Team" on page 2-13 for a detailed discussion.

Special Attachments

Special attachments do not perform service or tasks associated with shore party teams. They are normally retained under the control of the shore party team headquarters. Special attachments may include liaison personnel from the augmentation units attached to the shore party teams.

Shore Party Team

The shore party team provides CSS to a battalion landing team (BLT) landing across a designated (numbered) beach. It is subordinate to the shore party group. The nucleus of the team is drawn from the landing support platoon, landing support company, TSB and augmented as required to accomplish the specific shore party group's or shore party team's mission. The shore party team consists of a headquarters, shore platoon, service platoon, and

motor transport/heavy equipment platoon (see figure 2-13, on page 2-12).

The Marine component of the shore party team performs the following tasks:

- Marking limits of the beach unloading points.
- Designating and marking landing sites for helicopters.
- Locating and establishing multi-class supply dumps.
- Assisting the beach party in the landing and moving of units across the beach.
- Marking and removing obstacles in the BSA that are hazardous to personnel or may impede operations.
- Constructing and maintaining beach roads.
- Establishing and operating information centers.
- Maintaining current situation maps to assist landed units.
- Controlling traffic in the BSA.
- Maintaining communications with troop commanders of waterborne and helicopterborne assault units and the TACLOG for control purposes.
- Establishing lateral communications between beaches and HLZs.
- Marking contaminated/decontaminated portions of the BSA.
- Evacuating casualties and EPWs.
- Providing emergency maintenance for equipment in the waterborne assault.
- Maintaining continuous records, by category, of units, equipment, and amounts of supplies landed.
- Coordinating movement of amphibious vehicles carrying supplies.
- Loading/unloading supplies from landing craft, ships, and helicopters.
- Moving supplies to inland dumps or using units as required.
- Providing security and coordinating defense of the BSA.
- Initiating, as directed, civil affairs and military government activities in the BSA.

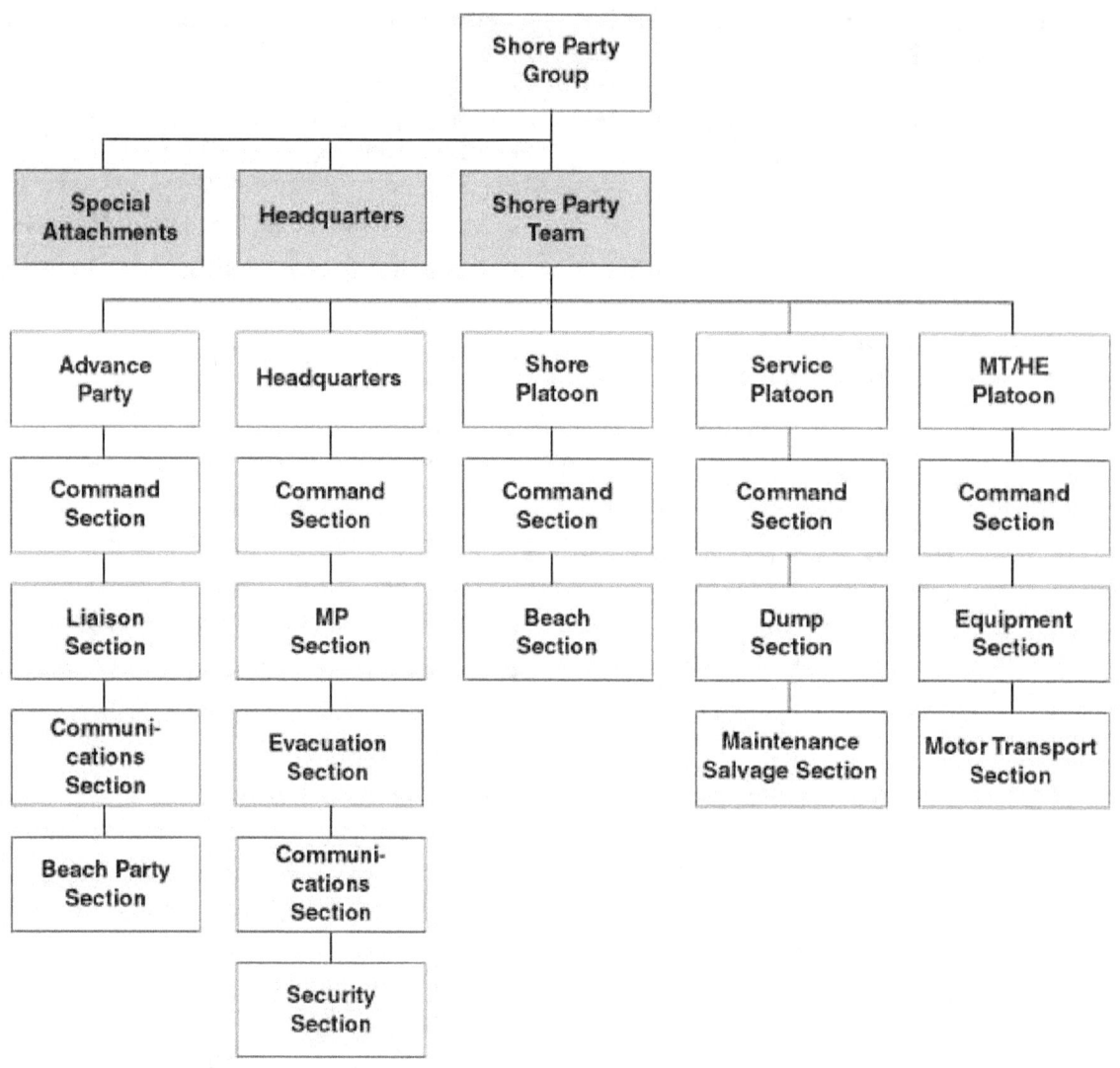

Note: The shaded areas indicate sections that are dissolved once the shore and beach party team headquarters land. The liaison section continues to operate with the BLT as an element of the shore party team headquarters.

Figure 2-13. Organization of a Typical Shore Party Team.

- Establishing and maintaining, as a part of the landing force warning system, a system to warn of air, ground, and NBC attacks within the BSA.

- Providing mortuary affairs services as directed.

- Constructing helicopter landing sites within the BSA.

- Establishing forward arming and refueling points (FARP) as required.

Advance Party. The advance party is composed of a command section, liaison section, communications section, and a beach party section. The advance party is a temporary organization. Its sole purpose is to effect a smooth transition ashore, and it is formed from the shore party team. The advance party conducts early beach reconnaissance, establishes communications, and marks landing sites and dumps before the remainder of the shore party team lands. The advance party sections return to their original units as the shore party team comes ashore (except liaison sections operating with the GCE).

Headquarters. The shore party team headquarters includes a command section, evacuation section, MP section, communications section, and security section. This section provides the C2 for the shore party team.

Shore Platoon. The shore platoon is a detachment from the shore party platoon and is augmented as required. The shore platoon organizes and operates the facilities for unloading supplies and equipment at the water's edge. It also organizes and operates the movement of material to the dump area or staging area or out of the BSA.

Service Platoon. The service platoon's nucleus comes from the shore party platoon and is augmented by specialists from CSS units. The service platoon organizes and operates dumps and maintenance/ salvage areas in the BSA.

Motor Transport/Heavy Equipment Platoon. The motor transport/heavy equipment platoon is drawn from primarily from TSB. This platoon provides equipment and motor transport support to the shore party team's sections and platoons.

Beach Party Group

The beach party group is the Navy counterpart to the shore party group. A beach party group is assigned to each designated beach and supervises, controls, and coordinates all Navy activities on that beach, such as boat salvage and lane clearing for landing craft. The beach party group includes a beach party group headquarters, beach party team(s), landing craft air

cushion (LCAC) craft landing zone (CLZ) control team(s), and a beach support unit (see figure 2-14).

The beach party group's mission is to provide the beach master, traffic control, causeway lighterage, causeways, ship-to-shore bulk fuel systems, limited construction capabilities, landing craft, and beach salvage capabilities. It also provides communications to C2 to its specially equipped teams. The beach party group facilitates the flow of troops, equipment, and supplies to the beaches and evacuates casualties, refugees, and EPWs as required.

Headquarters

The beach party group headquarters is drawn from the beach master unit of the NBG. The group commander and staff embark and land with the shore party group headquarters. The beach party group commander advises the shore party group commander on Navy matters, and they jointly plan for the expeditious use of all units employed in the BSA.

Beach Party Team

The beach party team is the Navy component to the shore party team and is commanded by a navy officer. The beach party team provides Navy functions (e.g., boat salvage, boat repair) for the shore party (see figure 2-15, on page 2-14).

Headquarters Section. The headquarters section contains the beach party team commander and communications and administrative assistants. A part of this team lands with the shore party team's advance party.

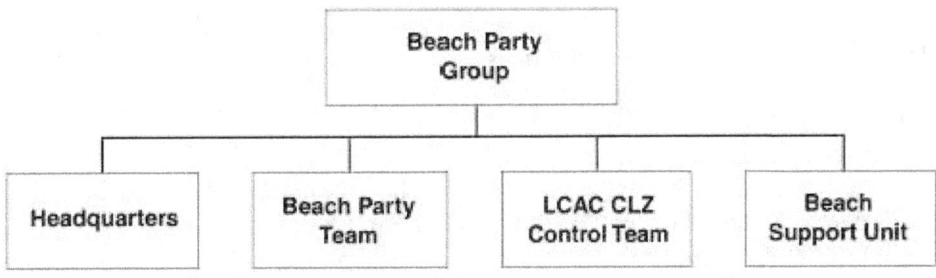

Figure 2-14. Beach Party Group.

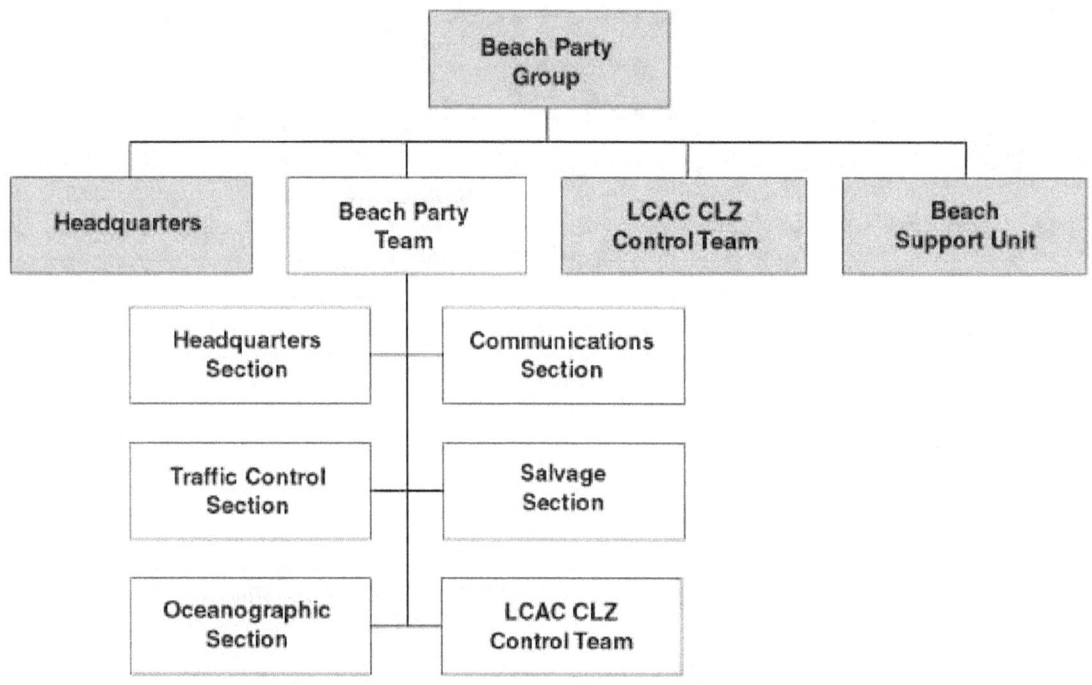

Figure 2-15. Beach Party Team.

Communications Section. The communications section contains personnel and equipment to transmit and receive operational information from various sources. This section uses lights, flags, and public address and broadcasting equipment to direct personnel and craft in the vicinity of the beach area. The communication section uses portable and mobile radio equipment to provide communications with units afloat and on adjacent beaches. It monitors the movement of landing craft's designated communications nets for beach touchdown points.

Traffic Control Section. The traffic control section, equipped with signal flags and other signal devices, controls traffic at unloading slots along the beach and directs beaching and retraction of craft.

Salvage Section. The salvage section contains personnel and equipment from the amphibious construction battalion and the NBG's beach master unit. This section assists the beaching and retraction of landing craft and ships, accomplishes minor beach improvement, and effects salvage of landing craft and amphibious vehicles. This section's equipment includes dozers, amphibious vehicles, and surf cranes. Landing craft may be assigned to this section to assist in boat salvage.

Oceanographic Section. The oceanographic section contains personnel drawn from the sea-air-land team, which is normally attached to the beach party group or beach party team. This section reports to the beach party team commander after completion of its tasks with the advance force. The oceanographic section performs tasks such as marking and removing obstacles in beach approaches up to the high watermark. It also performs hydrographic surveys and lifeguard duties, marks channels and navigational hazards, and improves seaward approaches. This section is equipped with inflatable boats, survey equipment, buoys, and demolitions.

LCAC CLZ Control Section. The duties and responsibilities of the LCAC CLZ control section are the same as the LCAC CLZ control team.

LCAC CLZ Control Team

The personnel for the LCAC CLZ control team come from the ship's complement. The LCAC CLZ control team controls LCACs as they approach the beach. This team directs the LCAC to a CLZ for unloading/loading, and then directs and controls the craft back to the ship. An LCAC CLZ support team supports each

LCAC CLZ control team. See Fleet Marine Force Manual (FMFM) 1-8, *Ship-to-Shore Movement,* for more detail.

Beach Support Unit

The beach support unit is drawn from the amphibious construction battalion of the NBG. This unit consists of a causeway platoon, fuels platoon, and camp support platoon (see figure 2-16). The beach support unit's primary mission is to provide causeway and fuel system support for the LFSP. Its secondary mission is to undertake military construction projects within the capabilities of assigned personnel and equipment. A beach support unit performs the following tasks:

- Installs causeway piers and uses causeway ferries to ferry equipment ashore.

- Provides capability to conduct ship causeway standoffs and compression marriages.

- Installs, operates, and maintains container over the shore systems.

- Installs and operates the roll-on/roll-off ship discharge facility.

- Installs, operates, and maintains amphibious assault fuel systems.

- Installs off shore petroleum, oils, and lubricants (POL) discharge systems.

- Provides beach salvage sections.

- Provides camp support and limited construction sections.

Special Attachments to Beach Party Group

Special attachments are attached to the beach party group to perform tasks or provide capability not normally included in the beach party organization. These attachments may provide support to the landing force, however, they typically perform Navy tasks that are more effective when performed from the beach.

Special Attachments to LFSP

There are many special attachments that may be made to the LFSP in order to perform the LFSP's assigned tasks. For example, units may be attached to the LFSP for defense or the landing force commander may deploy units to counter threats. The landing support commander may employ units operating in the BSA or landing zone support area (LZSA) in emergency situations, particularly in defense of the area.

Arrival and Assembly Operations Group

The AAOG is a task-organized group from the MAGTF whose function is to coordinate and control arrival and assembly operations (see figure 2-17 on page 2-16). It

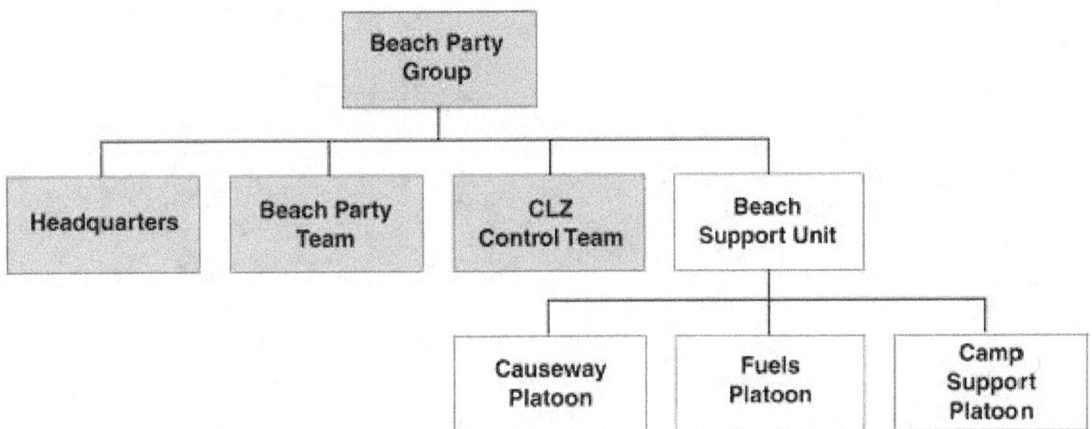

Figure 2-16. Beach Support Unit.

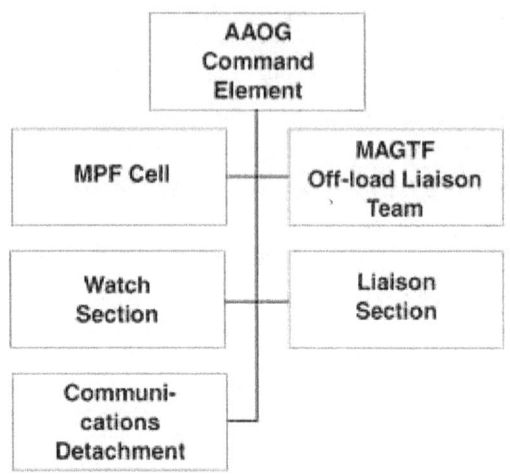

Figure 2-17. Notional AAOG Organization.

consists of personnel from all MAGTF elements plus liaison from the commander, naval support element (CNSE).

The AAOG—

- Monitors the airflow of the fly-in echelon (FIE) into the arrival and assembly area (AAA).

- Coordinates and monitors the throughput and distribution of maritime pre-positioned equipment and supplies (MPE/S) from the MPS to the unit assembly areas, specifically the arrival and assembly operations elements (AAOEs) within those assembly areas.

- Coordinates the association of MPE/S with designated organizations.

- Provides initial C2 functions for the MAGTF in the AAA.

- Directs and coordinates the AAOEs operations.

- Provides direction, coordination, and interface with the LFSP and airfield coordination officer (ACO) until such time as the respective MAGTF elements assume responsibility for those functions.

Tactical-Logistics Group

A parallel chain of command is established between the Navy and the MAGTF to conduct amphibious operations in accordance with JP 3-02, *Joint Doctrine for Amphibious Operations*. This chain of command allows the resolution of command and control issues at the lowest possible level. To effect this chain of command, the MAGTF establishes a TACLOG wherever a Navy ship-to-shore control organization is established. The TACLOG is the MAGTF's counterpart to the Navy's control organization. It is not part of the Navy ship-to-shore control organization; it is the MAGTF's liaison to the Navy. TACLOGs embark on the same ship as the Navy control officer exercising control over the ship-to-shore movement (see figure 2-18).

Mission

A MAGTF commander establishes TACLOGs as required. A TACLOG is a temporary task organization formed by the MAGTF, and it is composed of MAGTF personnel. It is concerned with both tactical and logistical ship-to-shore movement. A TACLOG's mission is to communicate MAGTF ship-to-shore movement requirements to the Navy's control organization and to assist the Navy in landing personnel, supplies and equipment in accordance with the MAGTF landing plan. The landing force TACLOG monitors the operations of subordinate TACLOGs and intervenes only if necessary to provide control/coordination at a higher level. TACLOGs link the LFSP, shore party, HST, and the Navy control organization. They also serve as the landing force commander's primary source of information concerning the status of MAGTF units during the ship-to-shore movement. FMFM 1-8 has detailed information concerning TACLOG.

Responsibilities

It is the collective responsibility of the Navy control organization, TACLOG, LFSP, and HST to—

- Know, at all times, what units are ashore and the status of any requests made for landing additional personnel, supplies, and/or equipment.

- Orchestrate and regulate movement of scheduled waves to ensure personnel, supplies, and equipment arrive at the designated location at the prescribed time and in the condition required to accomplish the assigned mission.

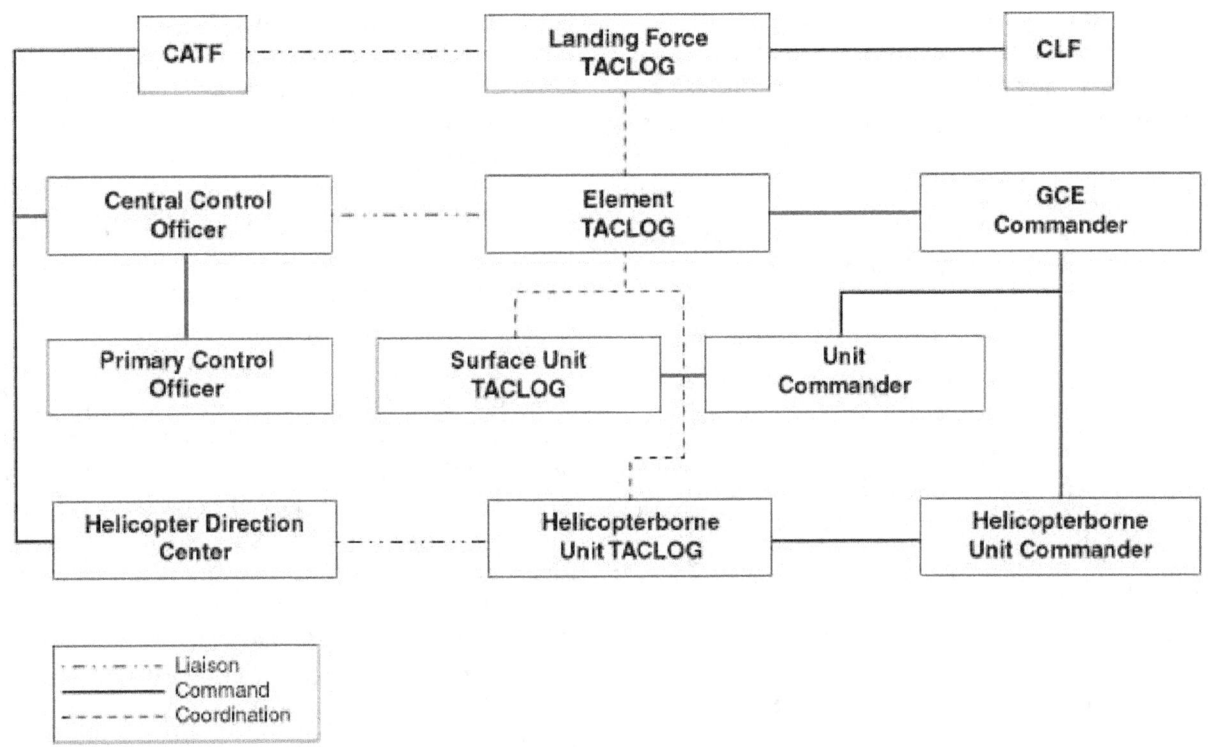

Note: "Element" can be read as GCE, ACE or CSSE. "Unit" can be any unit within the element.

Figure 2-18. Sample TACLOG Relationships.

- Ensure pre-positioned emergency supplies and floating dumps are responsive to the MAGTF's needs and moved rapidly to the designated location when required.
- Ensure on-call waves are prepared to move ashore rapidly to the designated location.
- Orchestrate preparations for nonscheduled waves to move ashore.

Based on the mission, TACLOG becomes the primary and critical link between the MAGTF and the Navy control organization, LFSP, and HST. The TACLOG must know the status of all phases of the ship-to-shore movement and the status of the LFSP, shore party, HST, and the Navy control organization.

Tasks

Each TACLOG, despite command level or specific focus, must be prepared to process requests and provide recommendations to Navy control organizations. TACLOGs must also be capable of performing the following tasks:

- Coordinating pre-D-day and pre-H-hour transfers involving landing force personnel and equipment.
- Monitoring scheduled waves.
- Providing information and recommendations to the Navy control organization to facilitate the landing of on-call and nonscheduled serials/waves.
- Processing and coordinating requests for support.
- Expediting, in coordination with the Navy control organization, the landing of personnel, supplies, and equipment in accordance with plans and orders.
- Advising the Navy control organization of the location of requested items.
- Recommending the type of landing craft or helicopter(s) required based on the tactical situation ashore and the availability of transportation assets.
- Anticipating requirements and coordinating the debarkation of nonscheduled serials.

- Advising the Navy control organization of the priority for landing serials during periods of congestion at the off-load site or when a shortage of transportation assets affects the tactical situations ashore.

- Advising the Navy control organization of changes in the landing sequence or landing plan and their effect on the tactical situation ashore.

- Maintaining records of the landing's progress. This includes the date-time-group (DTG) of scheduled, on-call, and nonscheduled serials; indicating those requested and those landed; and the current location of serials not yet landed.

- Sending/receiving periodic serial status reports to the landing force commander concerning the buildup ashore and other factors that may delay or change the landing plan.

- Coordinating with the Navy control organization to ensure that the ship's locations and movements do not conflict with MAGTF operations or communications.

- Monitoring the progress of tactical operations to anticipate requirements, coordinate the landing of nonscheduled and nonserialized sections, and recommend adjustments or deviations from the landing plan as required.

- Formulating decisions that may affect tactical operations ashore (within the limits of authority delegated to the TACLOG officer in charge [OIC]).

- Coordinating the buildup of supplies at BSAs and HLZs and/or combat service support areas (CSSAs) with the LFSP, HST, and other CSS organizations.

- Identifying landing requirements (landing craft/ helicopters).

- Maintaining records of the ship's location and informing the LFSP and HST commanders of changes as they occur.

- Coordinating and assisting in the control of withdrawal operations with the Navy control organization and ship's combat cargo officer as required.

Task Organization

The organization of each TACLOG varies to meet the requirements of a specific unit and operation. TACLOGs are composed of landing force tactical and logistical representatives. The landing force TACLOG is normally located aboard the amphibious force flagship. The basic organization is prescribed by the landing force commander and indicated in the MAGTF operation order. The landing force commander specifies which subordinate commanders are to organize and operate TACLOGs and ensures the TACLOG structure parallels the Navy control structure. If subordinate commanders are required to establish TACLOGs, their operation orders should specify the composition of their TACLOG.

Personnel assigned to the TACLOG must include both tactical and CSS personnel who are thoroughly familiar with MAGTF plans, Navy control procedures, and movement capabilities of both the Navy and the MAGTF. Representatives should include a G-3/S-3 (operations staff officer) representative (responsible for the TACLOG until the general off-load), a G-4/S-4 (logistic staff officer) representative (responsible for the TACLOG once the general off-load begins), a MAGTF/unit embarkation officer, a CSSE representative, communications personnel, administrative personnel, and liaison personnel from other units. Assigned personnel must possess a detailed knowledge of the operation order; embarkation order; CSS concept; ship's loading plans; tactical and CSS requirements; and plans, capabilities, and documents relating to the landing.

Helicopter Support Teams

Mission

The HST's mission is to facilitate the landing and movement of helicopterborne forces, equipment, and supplies to and within the landing zone. Normally, an HST is employed in each landing zone to provide support to units operating in and around that zone. An HST is formed for all helicopterborne operations. The HST also supports the evacuation of casualties and EPWs.

Once the HST is established in the landing zone, it assumes responsibility for helicopter terminal guidance from the reconnaissance unit. HST operations are terminated when the helicopterborne unit is no longer dependent on helicopter support as the primary means of support or when a combat service support buildup commences in the landing zone.

HST Organizational Structure

The HST is a task organization composed of personnel and equipment from the helicopterborne unit and the LFSP. It is augmented from other units as required. The actual organization and commander of the HST is decided by the helicopterborne unit commander. This decision is based on the mission and whether a combat service support buildup is planned for the area.

The HST normally consists of an advance party, headquarters, helicopter control section, and landing zone platoon (see figure 2-19). HST personnel must be fully trained and capable of carrying out their assigned duties (including the special considerations required of helicopterborne operations).

The MAGTF operation order specifies when control of the landing zone passes from the HST to the CSSE. Passing control can be specified by a specific time or event (i.e., when sufficient CSSE C2 capability is in the landing zone) or by order of the landing force commander.

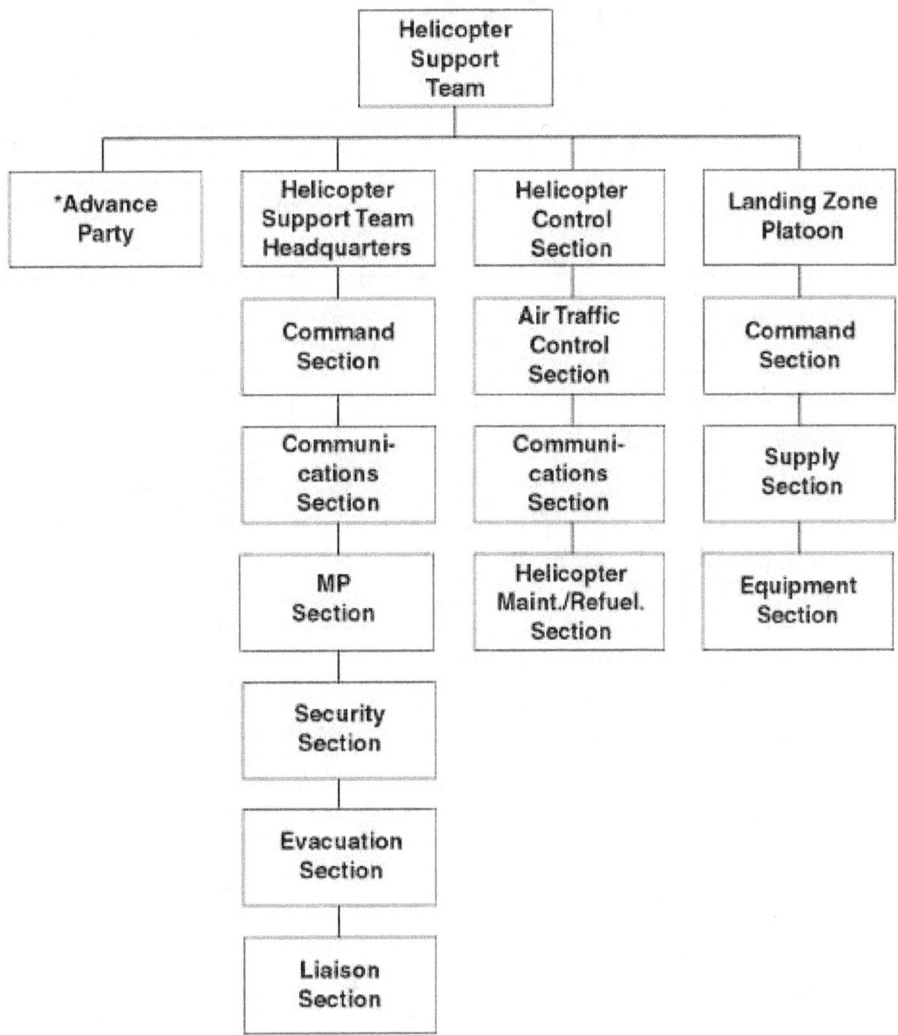

*Note: Advance party disbanded after arrival of HST headquarters.

Figure 2-19. Helicopter Support Team.

Advance Party

The advance party consists of eight to ten personnel drawn from each section of the HST. The advance party lands early, reconnoiters a site for the CSS installation, establishes the command post, and erects unloading point markers (appendix A). Communications personnel provide immediate communications. Landing zone control personnel control the helicopters operating within the zone. The OIC of the advance party assumes OPCON over the reconnaissance unit that provided the initial terminal guidance into the landing zone. The OIC retains control of the reconnaissance unit until the helicopter control section assumes responsibility. After the HST is established in the landing zone, the advance party disbands and its personnel revert to their parent section within the HST.

Helicopter Support Team Headquarters

If no CSS buildup is planned, the HST headquarters comes from the helicopterborne unit. If a CSS buildup is planned, the HST headquarters comes from the LFSP's or CSSE's landing support platoon, this simplifies transfer of control to the CSSE once the CSS buildup begins. The HST headquarters assumes control of the landing zone as rapidly as possible. The HST headquarters consists of—

- A command section provided by the appropriate platoon headquarters and augmented as required.

- A communications section provided by the communications platoon of the helicopterborne unit or from the shore party as appropriate.
- An MP section from the shore party.
- A security section for internal security of the landing zone. The security section is provided by the helicopterborne unit.
- An evacuation section provided by the medical section of the helicopterborne unit.
- The liaison section that accompanied the headquarters element of the helicopterborne unit.

Helicopter Control Section

The ACE provides personnel for the helicopter control section. The helicopter control section is generally organized into three sections: air traffic control, communications, and helicopter maintenance and refueling. The helicopter control section establishes and operates electronic and visual navigation aids that guide aircraft. It directs and controls helicopter operations within the landing zone.

Landing Zone Platoon

The landing zone platoon is provided by the same unit that provides the HST command section. The landing zone platoon is organized into command, supply, and equipment sections. If MHE is required in the landing zone or if helicopter slings and related equipment are required for external lifts, the equipment section is provided by the shore party because this type of equipment is not organic to combat units.

CHAPTER 3. TRANSPORTATION COMMAND AND CONTROL

Movement Control

The organizations and their movement control responsibilities described in this paragraph are applicable to marshaling, movement and deployment. Amphibious and maritime pre-positioning force (MPF) operations apply a transportation C2 structure tailored specifically to their specialized mission, which is detailed later in this chapter.

Movement control centers (MCCs) are agencies that plan, route, schedule, and control personnel, supplies, and equipment movements over LOCs (point of origin to POE, POD to final destination or movements within the AO).

Transportation management and movement control agencies must function the same during training exercises as they do during operations. In some cases, the agencies are permanent. For example, every MAGTF should have a full-time transportation section. For smaller MAGTFs, this may be no more than one or two Marines in the combat service support operations center. In other cases, movement control agencies are temporary. Battalions, squadrons, regiments, and aircraft groups establish temporary movement control centers when their organizations are moving. Local standing operating procedures (SOPs) establish the composition and procedures for MCCs. Figure 3-1 depicts the relationships between various commands, their movement control agencies, and supporting organizations during deployment of a MAGTF.

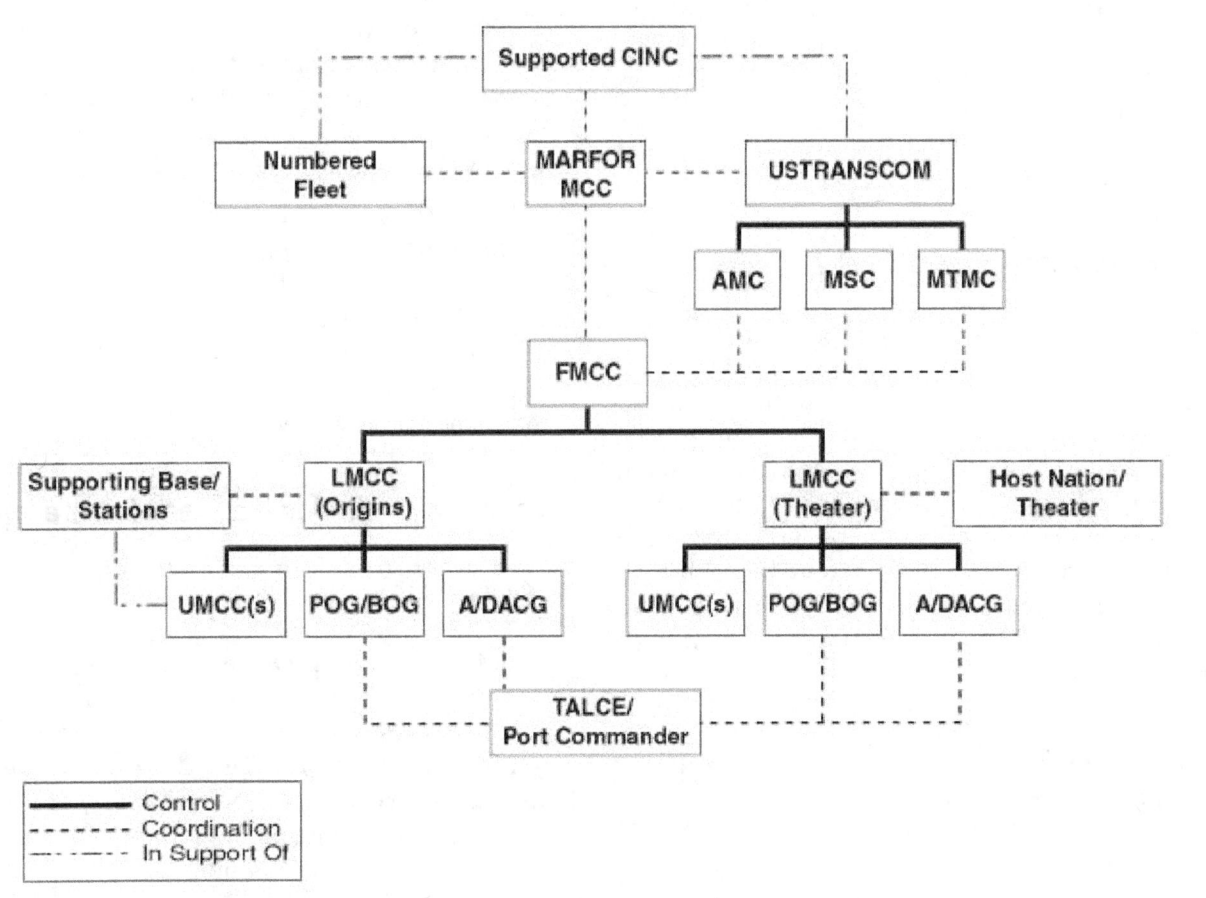

Figure 3-1. Movement Control Relationships During Deployment.

Movement Control Agencies

The following paragraphs describe movement control agencies during deployment.

Marine Force Headquarters' MCC

This is primarily an information processing agency to keep the Marine Corps forces (MARFOR) commander abreast of the status of subordinate unit deployments. This MCC can coordinate with the USTRANSCOM on transportation requirements, priorities, and allocations as required. When the MARFOR commander is operating in support of a JFC, the MARFOR's MCC coordinates with TRANSCOM via the JFC's JMC, which coordinates the requirements for all service components.

Force Movement Control Center

This is the MAGTF commander's agency to control and coordinate all deployment support activities. It is also the agency that coordinates with the transportation component commands (AMC, MTMC, MSC) of USTRANSCOM. When the MAGTF operates as part of a joint force under a JFC, the force movement control center (FMCC) coordinates with TRANSCOM via the JFC's JMC, which coordinates the requirements for all service components.

Logistic Movement Control Center

A CSSE or the supporting establishment(s) organize logistic movement control centers (LMCCs) near deploying units. The FMCC tasks the LMCC to provide organic or commercial transportation, transportation scheduling, MHE, and other support during marshaling and movement. The FSSG/CSSE can also establish two additional movement control organizations subordinate to the LMCC to support deployment: the arrival/departure airfield control group (A/DACG) and the port operations group (POG).

Major Subordinate Command Unit Movement Control Centers

The division, wing, and FSSG commanders provide forces to deploying MAGTFs. The commanders control transportation and communications assets needed to execute deployments. On order, each command activates its unit movement control center (UMCC) to support marshaling and movement.

Organizational UMCCs

Every deploying unit down to battalion/squadron/ separate company level activates a UMCC to control and manage its marshaling and movement.

Base Operations Support Group

Bases from which MARFOR units deploy establish base operations support groups to coordinate their efforts with those of the deploying units. Like MARFOR commands, bases have transportation, communications, and other assets useful to all commands during deployment.

Station Operations Support Group

Air stations from which MARFOR units deploy establish station operations support groups to coordinate their efforts with those of the deploying units. Like major MARFOR commands, air stations have transportation, communications, and other assets useful to all commands during deployment.

Flight Ferry Control Center

In addition to its MCC, the aircraft wing establishes a flight ferry control center to control deploying aircraft. The flight ferry control center operates under the cognizance of the MAW G-3.

Movement Control in the Area of Operations

Movement Control Center

The MCC is the primary agency in the AO to manage movement. As during deployments, lower echelon commands only activate MCCs while they are conducting movements. The MAGTF maintains an MCC during the entire deployment. It may be no more than the motor transport and embarkation staff officers. In joint and combined operations, the MAGTF MCC establishes liaison and communications with the theater MCC and other commands or host nations in whose areas it is operating.

Local SOPs

As with operations of MCCs during deployment, local SOPs establish the composition and procedures for MCCs. Figure 3-2 depicts relationships between various commands, their movement control agencies, and supporting organizations after arrival in the AO. The MAGTF commander often delegates responsibility for routine day-to-day movement control to the CSSE. Modifications to meet specific operational requirements are in the transportation appendix to annex D of the operation order.

MAGTF Movement Control Agencies

Movement control agencies in the AO are the same as in CONUS before deployment. Unit SOPs should be applicable during both deployment and employment.

Host-Nation Support

The MAGTF should use host-nation support transportation support to the maximum extent feasible, consistent with tactical considerations, to augment its organic capability.

Standardization Agreements

When operating in North Atlantic Treaty Organization (NATO) or quadripartite American, British, Canadian, and Australian Armies Standardization Program (ABCA), there are certain standardization agreements (STANAGs) among the participating nations by which the MAGTF is obligated to abide. These agreements are called STANAGs in the NATO arena and quadripartite standardization agreements (QSTAGs) in the ABCA arena.

Motor Transport Command and Control

The MAGTF commander and his subordinate commanders must exercise varying degrees of control

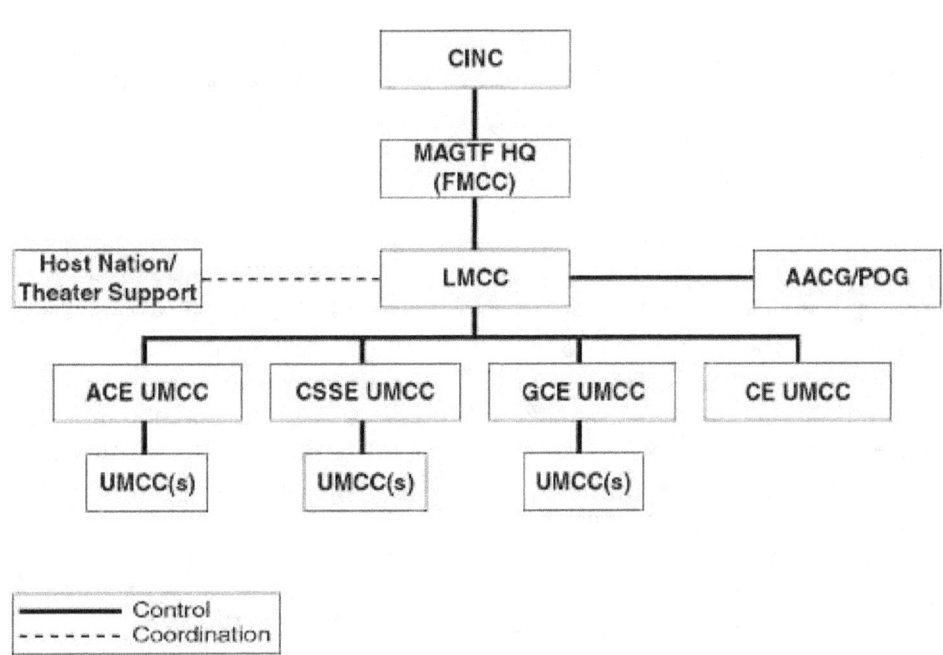

Figure 3-2. Movement Control Relationships in the AO/Theater.

over their motor transport assets before and during operations to ensure mission accomplishment.

Motor transport commanders plan and execute motor transport operations by assigning appropriate missions based on the concept of CSS, establishing appropriate command relationships, and supervising the flow of support.

Structure

CSSE motor transport units are task-organized. Transportation support tables of organization (T/Os) and tables of equipment (T/Es) are often subject to peacetime personnel and equipment-programming concerns and anticipated combat requirements. Transportation assets are limited; economy dictates proper prioritization and allocation. The motor transport commander task-organizes assets to support the main effort, as directed by the commander, while continuing to support the force as a whole. By task-organizing the MAGTF commander retains centralized control while providing for decentralized execution. Task-organizing promotes responsiveness.

Command Relationships

The first tool for exercising C2 is establishment of proper command relationships. A motor transport unit may remain under the control of its parent organization, allowing the motor transport commander to retain full authority over his organic units. This is not the only method. Motor transport units (both permanent and task-organized) can also be assigned to direct support (DS) of an organization other than their parent unit. Similarly, they can be attached to units other than their parent organizations. They may be attached to other CSSE(s), GCE, ACE or even to the forces of other armed Services. These options should always be considered during planning, keeping in mind that when motor transport units are assigned DS or attached to other organizations, centralized control is lost. The transportation commander no longer can assign or change the mission of units, which have been assigned DS or attached to other organizations. The transportation commander retains responsibility for supporting his units, which have been assigned DS to another commander.

Missions

Another tool that the transportation commander has available to control his assets is assignment of formal missions. The following paragraphs provide detailed information on the CSS missions and their associated responsibilities. These options give the commander flexibility across a spectrum ranging from fully centralized to decentralized control. The formalized mission structure facilitates changes by standardizing the responsibilities associated with each mission. When used in conjunction with structural options and command relationships, formally assigned support missions allow the commander to tailor transportation support to the specific tactical situation.

Transportation Missions

The concept of assigning formal missions to transportation units is intended to standardize CSS relationships, responsibilities, and C2 procedures. Clean, simple, and responsive lines of C2 are prerequisite to flexibility. Assignment of formal missions to transportation units improves support to the MAGTF from the inception of the operation to its termination. Assigning formal support missions to a transportation unit facilitates command and staff relationships; clarifies support relationships; and establishes liaison and communication responsibilities.

Mission Assignment

Formal CSS missions assigned by the CSSE commander to transportation units dictate specific responsibilities for the supporting transportation unit and the supported unit. For the unit, mission assignments establish not only the relationship to the supported force, but also the relationship to other support units. As shown in table 3-1, each of the three formal CSS missions has five inherent responsibilities:

- Priority of response to request.
- Area of responsibility.
- Liaison requirements.
- Establishment of communication.
- Locating/relocating.

Note: The terms DS and general support (GS), define specific responsibilities between supporting and supported units. They constitute a mission assignment and are given to a unit in paragraph 3b of the operations order. Attached constitutes a command relationship.

Table 3-1. Formal Combat Service Support Missions.

	CSS Missions	
	Direct Support	General Support
Responds to CSS requests in priority form:	Supported unit. HHQ CSSE or MAGTF. Own units.	HHQ CSSE or MAGTF. Supported unit. Own units.
Has as its tactical area of responsibility:	Area HHQ.	Area of supported unit.
Establishes liaison with:	Supported unit.	Supported unit.
Establishes communications with:	Supported unit. HHQ CSSE or MAGTF.	Supported unit. HHQ CSSE or MAGTF.
Positioned by:	HHQ CSSE or MAGTF in coordination with supported unit.	Higher CSS HQ.

Supporting Transportation Unit Responsibilities

Direct Support

Each unit assigned the mission of DS is immediately responsive to the needs of the designated supported element. It furnishes sustained support to that element and coordinates its operations to complement the concept of operations of the supported element. The essential feature of the DS mission is the one-to-one relationship between supporting and supported units. The DS mission is a decentralized formal mission. A unit assigned this mission—

- Responds to request for support, in order of priority, from its supported unit first, then from its higher headquarters, and finally from its subordinate units. In the event of conflicting requests, support to the supported unit takes precedence.
- Has as its AOR the supported unit's AO.
- Establishes communications with the supported unit and higher headquarters.
- Is positioned by higher headquarters in coordination with the supported unit. Positioning must complement the overall mission and consider the needs of the supported unit.

General Support

A mission of GS provides transportation support to the MAGTF under the direction of the MAGTF or CSSE headquarters. This mission provides responsive support to the requirements of the supported commanders. However, the CSSE commander retains control of the prioritization of tasks. The GS mission is the most centralized tactical mission. A unit assigned this mission—

- Responds to transportation requests, in priority, from supported units and CSS units.
- Has as its AOR the HHQ's AO.
- Establishes liaison as required by the operational situation with the supported units.
- Establishes communications with the supported unit and higher headquarters.
- Is positioned by higher headquarters. If there is no higher headquarters direction, it positions itself to best support the supported commander's concept of operations.

Attached

When attached and subject to limitations imposed in the attachment order, the commander of the unit or organization receiving the transportation attachment will exercise the same degree of C2 as over organic units. The responsibility for transfer and promotion of personnel will normally be retained by the parent organization.

Supported Unit Responsibilities

Requirements

Determination and identification of transportation requirements that exceed the organic capabilities of the supported unit are the responsibility of the supported unit in coordination with the supporting CSSE. Identification of requirements is the first step in the process of obtaining transportation support.

In the requirements determination process, the supported unit commander must evaluate his assigned mission, the situation, task organization, organic equipment capabilities and density, and the concept of operations. The supported unit commander must fully use organic motor transport assets before requesting transportation support. The CSSE commander must be engaged in the process to assist the supported unit. This enhances the CSSE commander's ability to anticipate demand.

A transportation support requirement generates a request to move specific quantities of cargo or personnel. The request is not a request for specific types or quantities of vehicles unless the tactical situation drives such a request. The supporting transportation unit commander will determine types and quantities of vehicles to support the requirement. Additionally, effective communications must be maintained between the supported unit and the supporting unit to establish requirements, priorities, and allocation of resources.

Prioritization

The supported unit commander should establish priorities well in advance so that the supporting unit can develop a complementary concept of support. Priorities, however, cannot be dealt with in a vacuum. Many other considerations dictate how the transportation unit will do its job.

Allocation of Resources

During planning, the supported unit commander must establish priorities and allocations. When prioritizing, the commander establishes the precedence of who and what. When allocating, the commander establishes how much.

Transportation C2 in Amphibious/Landing Support Operations

The LFSP's success lies in its ability to C2 its support elements on the beach, at the port, and in the landing zone. To establish an effective C2 system, the LFSP must integrate into the amphibious force's C2 systems. See JP 3-02, JP 3-02.1, *Joint Doctrine for Landing Force Operations*, JP 3-02.2, *Joint Doctrine for Amphibious Embarkation*, FMFM 1-8, and FMFM 4-2, *The Naval Beach Group*, for detailed C2 information.

Shore Party and Beach Party Teams

The shore party team commander controls and coordinates landing support activities within the assigned numbered, color-designated beach (e.g., red 1). Normally, the shore party team commander lands with the shore party team's advance party. The shore party team commander remains on the beach to initiate control and coordination of all landing support tasks.

The beach party team commander lands with the shore party team commander and is under the OPCON of the shore party team commander until the beach party group commander assumes control of the beach party.

Shore Party and Beach Party Groups

The shore party group commander controls and coordinates shore party activities within a designated colored beach (typically, a color designates the beach for a regimental landing team). This may include two or more numbered beaches (e.g., blue 1, blue 2). Once the shore party group commander lands, he assumes control of subordinate shore party team activities. The shore party group commander is the operational commander for both the shore party teams and the beach party group. The shore party group commander also begins to consolidate activities at the group level. Consolidation activities include—

- Redistributing shore party team personnel and equipment as required.
- Establishing shore party group communications and consolidation of existing shore party team communications.

- Sending liaison personnel to supported unit headquarters.

- Coordinating defensive measures.

- Coordinating beach party functions with the beach party group commander.

- Submitting reports and records.

The beach party group commander assumes control of the beach party teams after the beach party group lands. The beach party group commander remains under the OPCON of the shore party group commander until the CSSE lands and absorbs the shore party groups; then, the beach party commander assumes responsibility for beach party operations.

Landing Force Support Party

The LFSP commander controls and supervises landing support operations as set forth in the Combat Service Support Control Agencies Plan tab E to appendix 14 (Amphibious Operations) to annex C (Operations) of the operation order. The LFSP command element ensures success of landing support through close coordination, timely reinforcement, and consolidation of CSS activities. The LFSP commander moves the LFSP command post ashore once the situation allows.

The LFSP commander establishes the LFSP headquarters ashore and assumes OPCON of the shore party, beach party, and other LFSP units ashore. The shore and beach party commanders retain ADCON of their respective units (see figure 3-3). The LFSP headquarters' personnel and equipment that accompany the LFSP commander ashore should be minimal since the LFSP commander will use existing assets of the shore party headquarters to coordinate with the CLF and commander, amphibious task force (CATF).To avoid duplication, the shore and beach party headquarters become part of the LFSP C2 system.

Helicopter Support Team

The HST commander controls and coordinates all landing support activities within the assigned LZSA. The HST commander normally lands with the HST advance party.

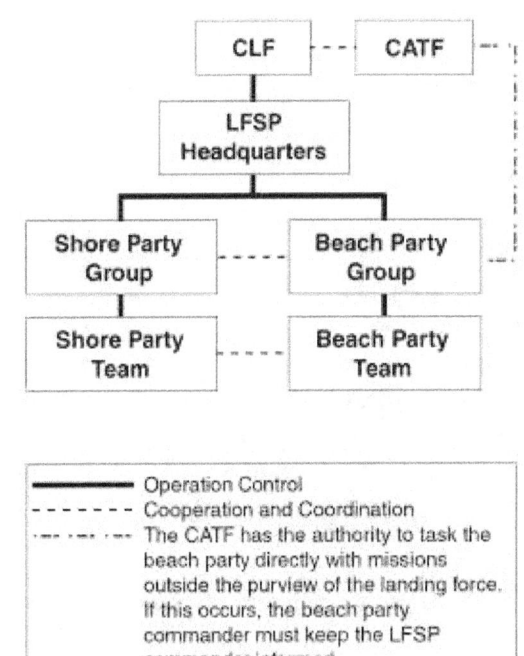

Figure 3-3. Final Command and Control Relationship.

Once HST operations in support of the helicopterborne unit initial insertion cease, the LFSP assumes responsibility for sustainment of the helicopterborne unit and operation of the associated LZSA. Those HST units previously attached to the helicopterborne unit return to OPCON of the LFSP.

Reports and Records

Reports and records are crucial to establish and maintain C2 during the initial phase of an amphibious assault. Reports provide the status of the movement, personnel, and supplies ashore. It is essential that the LFSP provide the landing force commander with the status of units ashore. This information becomes a basis for the commander's tactical decisions. The reports' paragraph or report tab to the landing force support party appendix to annex D (Logistics/Combat Service Support) of the operation order identifies the required content and time of submission of LFSP reports. The required reports vary with each operation.

Subordinate units of the shore party and HST maintain and must continually update unit and equipment movement records. These records are submitted to higher headquarters where they are consolidated with other applicable material to develop the required reports. The following paragraphs discuss some of the records that must be maintained.

Beach (Landing Zone) Support Area Overlay

This overlay shows the location and disposition of all units, combat service support dumps, unloading points, command posts, landing support units, bivouac areas, temporary bivouacs in the BSA, LZSA, road net, traffic control plans, and landing support installations.

Beach (Landing Zone) Defense Overlay

This overlay shows the defensive organization of the support area. All organizations assigned a ground defensive mission in the support area are shown, even if they are not organic to the shore party team or HST. This overlay is submitted to the next higher landing support echelon and the supported unit commander as soon as possible. Changes are reported as they occur.

Tactical Situation Overlay

Since the shore party/HST requires security and protection during a landing, it is essential that the shore party/HST be aware of the tactical situation. The tactical situation overlay identifies the tactical disposition of all friendly forces and aids in the delivery of CSS. The tactical situation overlay is also used to brief arriving unit commanders on the latest tactical situation.

Enemy Situation Overlay

This overlay shows the location of enemy forces in the objective area. It is used to identify the current enemy situation for the shore party/HST commanders and to orient unit commanders passing through the area.

Disposition to Seaward Chart

This chart shows the location and disposition of friendly naval units. It includes picket boats and off-shore transfer barges.

Ships' Position Chart

This chart indicates the relative position of each ship that is or will be unloaded by a shore party echelon.

Ships' Unloading Status Chart

This chart provides the LFSP commander with the unloading status of each transport/cargo ship. It also provides unit commanders and their staffs with the status of their troops and gear. The ships' unloading status chart includes—

- Percentage of personnel unloaded.
- Percentage of vehicles unloaded.
- Percentage of cargo, by class, unloaded.
- Estimated percentage of entire ship unloaded.
- Estimated time of completion to unload entire ship.
- Ship's scheduled time of return to the sea echelon.

Dump Status Chart

This chart reflects quantity of supplies received, issued, and on hand at a specified time.

Casualty and EPW Evacuation Chart

This chart shows the number of casualties and EPWs received, evacuated, and retained.

Vehicle and Equipment Status Chart

This chart provides the disposition of vehicles and equipment operating under control of the LFSP.

LFSP Personnel Distribution Chart

This chart shows personnel attached to the LFSP by unit and their deployment to subordinate landing support units.

Serials Landed Status Report

This report records the status of equipment and personnel who have reached their intended designated beach.

Communications

To maintain C2, the LFSP must communicate with each of its units, the TACLOG, and ships participating in the landing. A reliable, flexible, and effective communications net is essential to C2 because it allows the commander to monitor the status of the LFSP.

Note: TACLOGs monitor ship-to-shore movement and provide the CATF and CLF with critical information concerning the movement and forces ashore.

As soon as advance units of the shore party or HST land, they establish primary and alternative communications nets. Alternative communications nets generally parallel beachmaster communications nets and are used if the primary communications net fails. After advance units have landed and established communications, they relay requests for troop serials and supplies from the commanders ashore to the TACLOGs located on the control ships. All requests for troop serials and supplies are made via the LFSP, except when LFSP communications are not established. If the urgency of the situation or the failure of a communications net requires the landing force to transmit its requirements directly to the TACLOG through a tactical or command net, the landing force must notify the LFSP immediately upon reestablishment of communications.

The shore party/HSTs are the primary users of communications equipment, messengers, wire, facsimiles, radios, and supplementary (visual and sound) communications because they must communicate with the ship, landing craft, and aircraft. In addition to standard communications equipment, the LFSP uses supplementary communications (e.g., public address systems, electronic megaphones, various signal lights) to direct the landing and movement of crafts in and around the beaches and the HLZ. See MCWP 6-22 for specific communications information.

Beach and Landing Site Markers

The use of beach and landing site markers is another method to maintain control. Standard markers are used by the shore party teams and the HSTs to maintain order and to facilitate smooth operations ashore. Markers locate and identify beaches, landing sites, unloading points, dumps by class of supplies, beaching points for landing ships, range markers, landing points for vehicles, and casualty evacuation points. Standard markers are available to support both day and night operations. Appendix A contains illustrations of standard beach and landing site markers.

Transportation C2 in MPF Arrival and Assembly Operations

Maritime pre-positioning provides a combatant commander with deployment flexibility and increased capability to respond rapidly to crisis or contingency with a credible force. The purpose of an MPF operation is to rapidly establish a MAGTF ashore to conduct subsequent operations across the operational continuum. An MPF operation may consist of one ship and an appropriate sized MAGTF or all maritime pre-positioning ships squadrons (MPSRONs).

Arrival and Assembly

Arrival and assembly may well be the most crucial phase of an MPF operation and includes—

- Initial preparation of the AAA.
- Coordinated arrival and off-load of equipment and supplies from the MPSRON (in port, across a beach or both).
- Reception of the FIE.
- Movement and distribution of the MPE/S.
- Security.
- Preparation for the MAGTF operational mission.

Commencement and Disestablishment

The arrival and assembly phase begins on arrival of the first maritime pre-positioning ship or the first aircraft of the main body at the designated AAA. This phase ends when adequate equipment and supplies are off-loaded and issued to awaiting units, C2 communications are established, and the MAGTF commander reports that all essential elements of the MAGTF have attained combat readiness. Simultaneous or subsequent tactical operations by the

MAGTF and movements to those operations are not considered part of the MPF operation.

Arrival and Assembly Organizations

MPF C2 organizations and their relationships for arrival and assembly are depicted in figure 3-4.

Arrival and Assembly Operations Group

The AAOG is a task-organized group from the MAGTF whose function is to coordinate and control arrival and assembly operations. It consists of personnel from all MAGTF elements plus liaison from the CNSE. The AAOG must—

● Monitor the airflow of the FIE into the AAA.

● Coordinate the association of MPE/S with designated organizations.

● Provide initial C2 functions for the MAGTF in the AAA.

● Direct and coordinate the AAOE's operations.

● Provide direction, coordination, and interface with the LFSP and ACO until such time as the respective MAGTF elements assume responsibility for those functions.

● Publish the daily situation report.

Arrival and Assembly Operations Element

Each element within the MAGTF and Navy support element (NSE) establishes an AAOE to perform the following tasks:

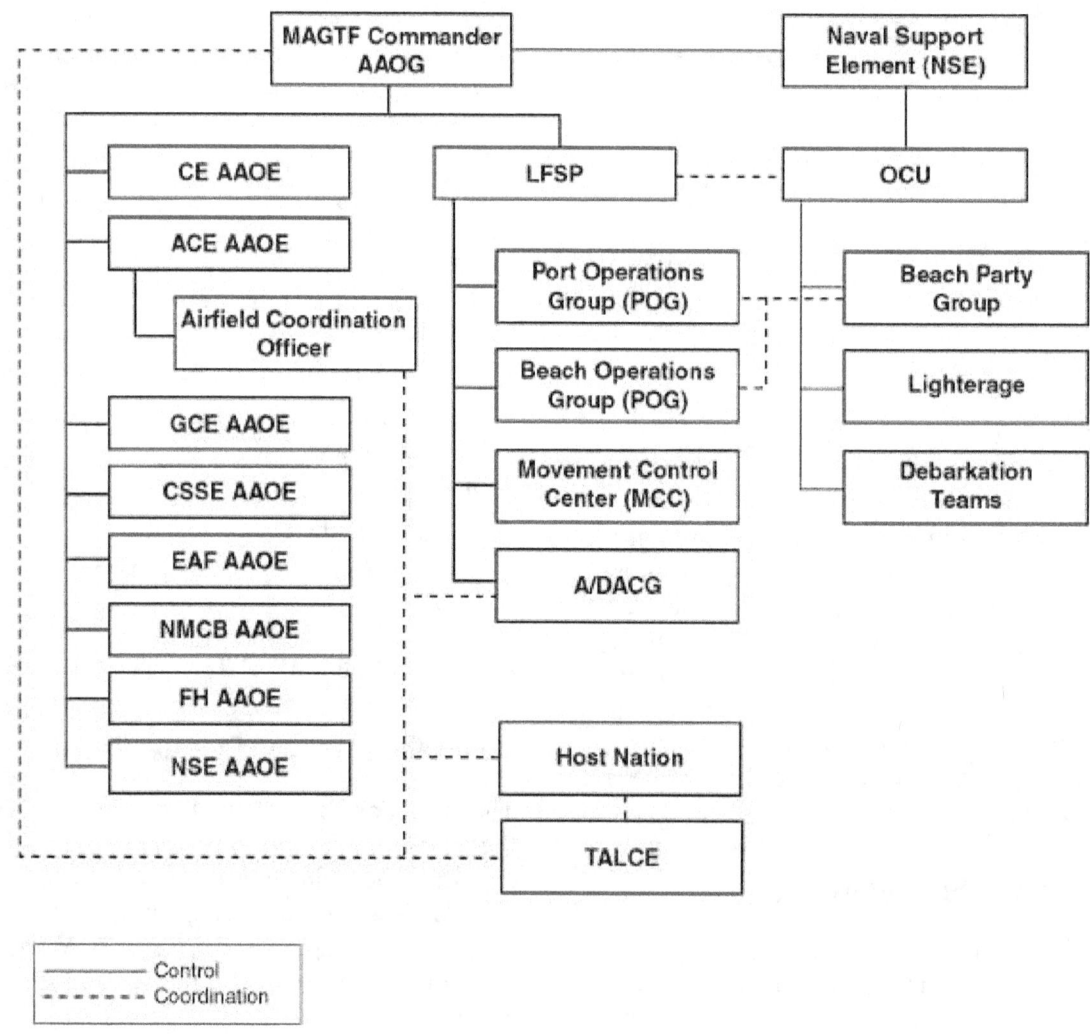

Figure 3-4. C2 Organizations for Arrival and Assembly.

- Provide initial C2 activities within the assembly area until arrival of the element commander.

- Receive MPE/S and verify items with the MAGTF. Distribute MPE/S to unit equipment reception points (ERPs) per the MAGTF commander's distribution plan.

- Provide liaison with the AAOG.

- Coordinate security in the assembly areas.

- Oversee preparations for combat.

- Provide throughput reports to the AAOG as directed by the arrival and assembly plan.

Airfield Coordination Officer

The airfield coordination officer is designated by the MAGTF commander under the cognizance of the ACE and acts as the single point of contact for host-nation support and other support peculiar to aviation operations at the airfield(s). Non-Air Mobility Command support requirements identified by the tanker airlift control element (TALCE) advanced echelon will be coordinated through the airfield coordination officer. The airfield coordination officer should be a member of the survey, liaison, and reconnaissance party (SLRP) to facilitate airfield operational planning.

Landing Force Support Party

The LFSP is a task-organized unit composed primarily of elements from the CSSE and NSE augmented by other MAGTF elements. The LFSP controls throughput of personnel and MPE/S at the port, beach, and airfield. The LFSP falls under the control of the OIC, AAOG and has four principal throughput groups:

- POG.

- Beach operations group (BOG).

- AACG.

- MCC.

Port Operations Group

The POG is a task-organized group from the MAGTF's beach and terminal operations unit and the Navy cargo handling force. The POG may be retained after arrival and assembly for the off-load of resupply shipping as well as retrograde of damaged equipment. The POG is responsible for preparing the port prior to arrival of the maritime pre-positioning ship and the throughput of supplies and equipment as they are off-loaded from the ship. The POG operates under the overall direction of the LFSP and in coordination with the ship's debarkation officer. The POG is responsible for the following tasks:

- Establish overflow areas for supplies and equipment.

- Clear piers and overflow areas of material.

- Establish communications with the LFSP and ship's debarkation officer.

- Establish liaison with host-nation port authorities for employment of cargo and material handling equipment, operations and longshoreman support, and dunnage.

- Operate cargo/materials handling equipment including shore-based cranes, forklifts, tractors, dollies, lighting, etc.

- Assist Navy cargo handling force detachments in ship off-load as directed and transport cargo to overflow areas as necessary.

- Establish bulk fuel/water reception and transfer facilities as directed.

- Be prepared to continue port operations for follow-on shipping.

Beach Operations Group

The BOG is a task-organized group from the MAGTF landing support unit and the NSE. The BOG operates under the overall direction of the LFSP and in coordination with the assault craft unit. The BOG may be retained after the arrival and assembly for the off-load of follow-on shipping.

The functions of the BOG and associated NSE beach party teams (BPTs) include:

- Providing the beach area C2 necessary to control and coordinate the throughput of MPE/S.
- Organizing and developing the beach area as necessary to support the throughput of MPE/S, to include designating and establishing overflow areas.
- Coordinating the bulk fluid transfer as required.
- Off-loading lighterage at the beach.
- Providing direction for MAGTF drivers to move vehicles from the lighterage.
- Providing surge vehicle operators.
- Preparing for follow-on operations.

Arrival Airfield Control Group

The AACG is responsible for the control and coordination of the off-load of airlifted units and equipment and provides limited combat service support to those units. The AACG is task-organized around a nucleus provided by the landing support company of the CSSE and is structured and manned to provide continuous operations support for multiple aircraft. Normally, the AACG will deploy as an element of the advance party and initiate operations at the arrival airfield. AACG is the point of contact between TALCE at the arrival airfield and the LFSP.

Movement Control Center

The MCC is the agency that plans, routes, schedules, and controls personnel and equipment movements over LOCs. In MPF operations, the MCC forms the MPE/S being off-loaded from the ship or aircraft into separate AAOE convoys for movement to the AAOEs (see figure 3-5).

Automated Information Systems Support

MAGTF II/Logistics Automated Information System

The MAGTF II/logistics automated information system (MAGTF II/LOG AIS) family of systems

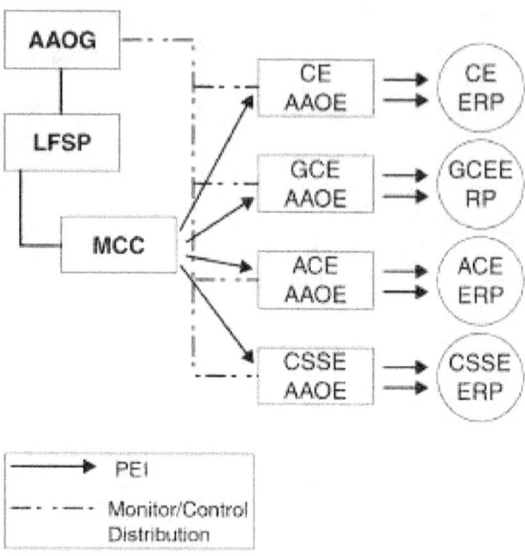

Figure 3-5. Movement Control Center Relationships.

provides the automated information support necessary to assist in the control of transportation operations.

MAGTF II/LOG AIS is a family of coordinated, mutually supporting, automated systems designed to support deliberate and crisis action/time-sensitive planning, deployment, employment, and redeployment of a MAGTF in independent, joint and/or multinational operations. MAGTF II/LOG AIS is composed of interrelated systems that perform common and discrete functions (see figure 3-6). It also includes the MAGTF Data Library (MDL), which serves as source data for the systems.

Each system shares a common database, yet performs separate and complementary functions. Each of the systems uses the same data and, if so desired, the same plan. This allows a plan (see figure 3-7 and figure 3-8, on page 3-14) to go through the various stages of creation, sourcing, assignment to transportation assets and time-phased force deployment data (TPFDD) construction without the necessity of exporting data from one system to another.

MAGTF II

MAGTF II is used by the Marine Corps planning community to create contingency and execution operations plans. Additionally, MAGTF II acts as the Marine Corps' TPFDD interface with the Joint Operations Planning and Execution System (JOPES).

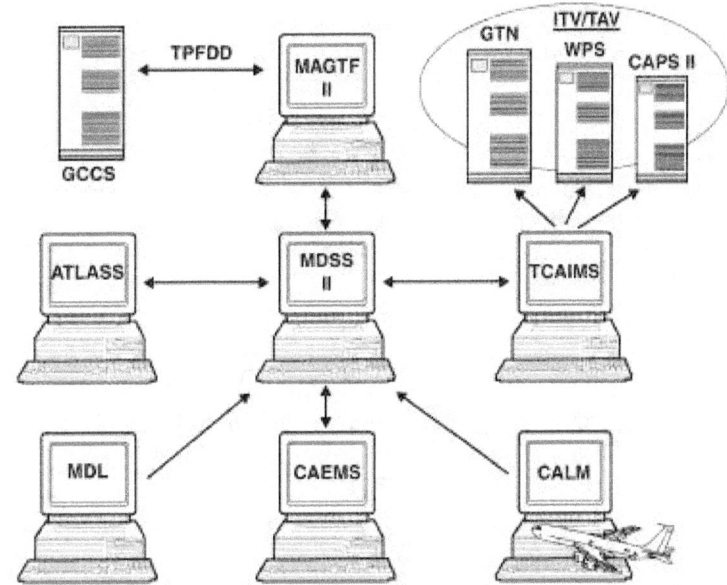

Figure 3-6. MAGTF II LOG AIS Relationships.

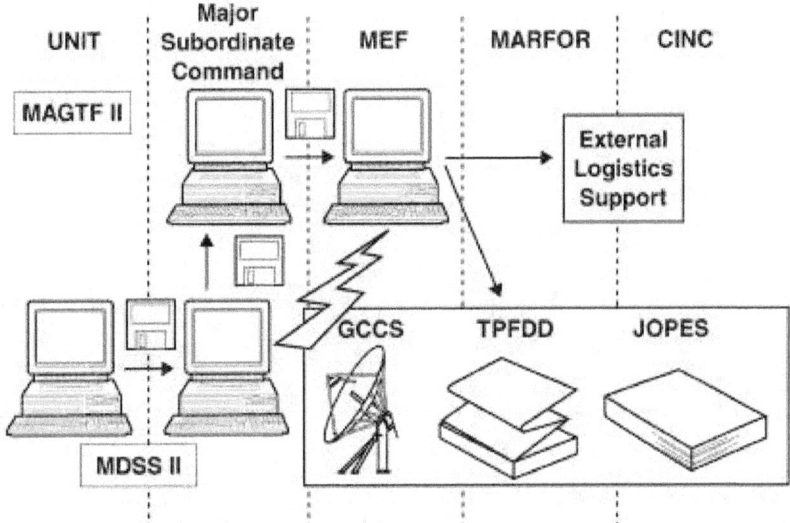

Figure 3-7. MAGTF II and MDSS II Planning.

Used primarily in the planning and marshalling phases of operations, MAGTF II provides the information and functionality necessary to—

- Forecast lift and sustainability requirements.

- Provide deployment requirements to MAGTF Deployment Support System II (MDSS II) for detailed sourcing and refinement at the battalion, squadron or separate company level.

- Rapidly develop and refine TPFDD information to meet crisis planning based on combatant commander and service-mandated deadlines.

- Compare and select alternative force structures.

- Allow the rapid sharing of detailed deployment information between planners, operators, and logisticians.

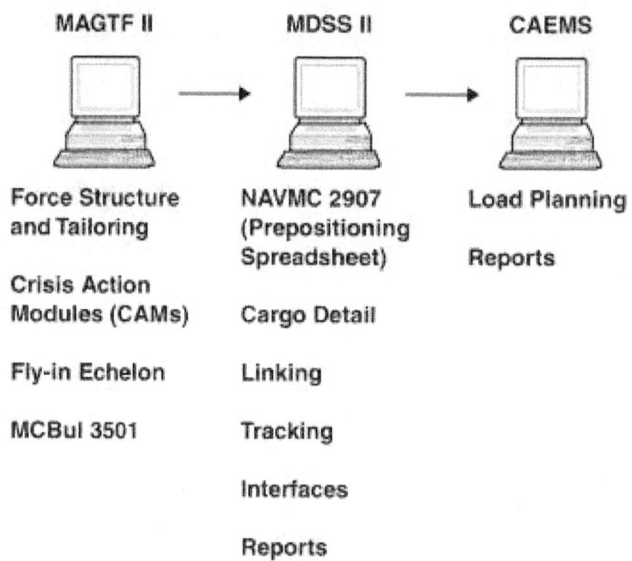

Figure 3-8. MPF Functions.

Note: MAGTF II is to be replaced by the joint force requirements generator II as part of the JOPES 2000 upgrade. No specific date for project termination has been set.

MDSS II

MDSS II is the unit-level (battalion/squadron/separate company) deployment planning and execution system that provides MAGTF and subordinate elements a single source automated deployment database. See figures 3-9 and 3-10. MDSS II provides commanders with the ability to respond to MAGTF II taskings for detailed plan data. Used during all phases of an MPF operation, MDSS II provides the information and functionality necessary to—

- Source and tailor plan-specific force structures composed of personnel, equipment, and supplies for multiple operation plans.

- Monitor embarkation readiness status.

- Provide movement and embarkation planning data.

- Assign pre-positioned assets and equipment to specific units.

- Develop and tailor equipment databases for future operations.

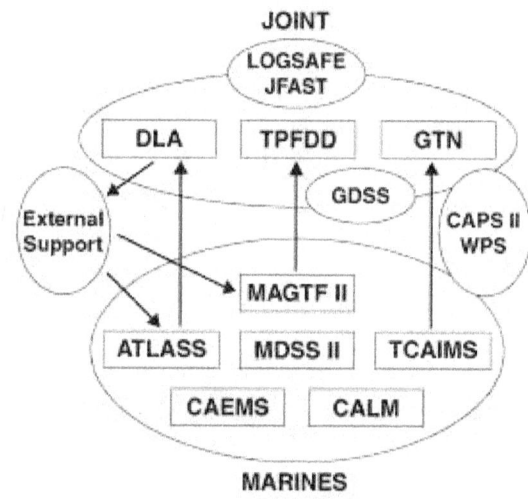

Figure 3-9. Deployment Systems Overview.

- Use logistics applications of automated marking and reading symbols (LOGMARS) for barcoding and scanning to—

  - Create labels.

  - Rapidly associate containers/vehicles and their contents.

  - Update cargo and equipment date, time, and location in the MDSSII database by downloading data directly from the LOGMARS data collection devices (DCDs) or transmitting real time from the DCD via wireless modem.

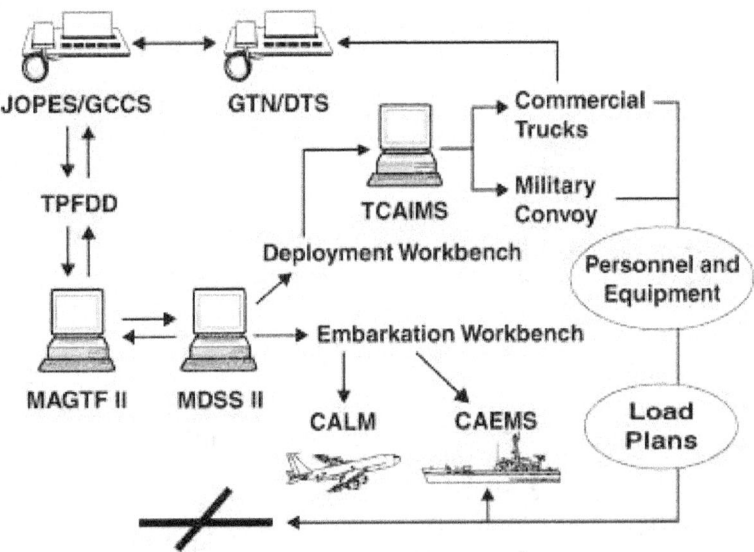

Figure 3-10. Deployment Support.

- Track equipment and supplies from ship to shore and through phases of an off-load with near-real-time updates.

- Create supply transactions that update asset tracking for logistics and supply system (ATLASS) in order to create accountability records.

- Provide unit-level movement requirements information to Transportation Coordinator's Automated Information for Movement System (TCAIMS) for determination and assignment of transportation from origin to POE and POD to destination.

- Provide unit-level embarkation data to computer-aided embarkation management system (CAEMS) and computer aided load manifesting (CALM) systems in order to prepare load plans.

- Provide standard and ad hoc reports in response to information requests.

- Provide equipment density lists to the Supported Activity Supply Systems (SASSY) management unit (SMU) to develop Class IX and secondary repairable requirements for using units.

CAEMS

CAEMS is used by the unit-level embarkation officer to accomplish detailed load planning of Amphibious and Military Sealift Command shipping and produce supporting documentation. CAEMS provides the information and functionality necessary to—

- Template deck diagrams for both amphibious and Military Sealift Command shipping.

- Produce dangerous cargo manifests.

- Conduct trim, stress, and stability calculations.

- Produce 'as loaded' deck diagrams upon completion of loading.

Note: CAEMS is to be replaced by the Integrated Computerized Deployment System (ICODES) in the future.

TCAIMS

Transportation coordinators (i.e., LMCC and motor transportation coordinators) use TCAIMS to manage transportation assets in the deployment, employment, and redeployment of operational forces.

TCAIMS provides the information and functionality necessary to—

- Manage requests, tasking, and dispatching associated with daily transportation operations at all levels of command.

- Plan, coordinate, and manage transportation assets from origin to POE and from POD to destinations.

- Provides the source data that feeds USTRANSCOM and the Defense Transportation System (DTS) to facilitate in-transit visibility (ITV).

Note: MDSS II and TCAIMS will migrate to the joint system, TCAIMS II. No project termination date has been set.

Supporting Systems

The following are non-MAGTF II/LOG AIS systems that provide support to transportation operations.

MAGTF Data Library

The MDL serves both data distribution and data quality control functions. Issued on a quarterly basis, this CD-ROM transmitted data set updates the permanent technical data files within MAGTF II/LOG AIS. The users of MAGTF II/LOG AIS are provided an opportunity to submit requests to change or correct this data through the use of a Data Trouble Report which is passed, via the logistics chain, to the contractor tasked with maintaining the MDL.

Computer Aided Load Manifesting

A U.S. Air Force-developed and -maintained system, CALMS provides a PC-based, automated tool for producing aircraft load plans. Selected data elements are exported from MDSS II to CALMS for load planning and lift estimation.

Note: CALMS is slated to be replaced by the joint system, Automated Aircraft Load Planning System (AALPS) in the future.

Fleet Optical Scanning Ammunition Marking System

Fleet optical scanning ammunition marking system (FOSAMS) is a PC-based automated system that tracks ammunition, creates government bills of lading (GBLs), and continuation sheets. FOSAMS also provides source data for dangerous cargo manifests as well as interfacing with MDSS II.

Note: FOSAMS is slated to be replaced by the U.S. Army managed Retail Ordnance Logistics Management System (ROLMS).

Retail Ordnance Logistics Management System

ROLMS is a comprehensive system that can perform all ammunition logistics management and reporting functions, such as inventory, requisitioning, issues, expenditures, receipts, asset maintenance, notice of ammunition reclassification processing, and transaction reporting.

War Reserve System

This mainframe system is used to compute sustainment and war reserve requirements for deliberate planning and crisis execution purposes in support of the various regional contingencies requiring Marine forces involvement. During deliberate planning, sourced requirements from the system flow into other MAGTF II information systems with the ultimate result of updating TPFDDs for various contingencies. In the event of contingency operations, materiel release transactions generated within the war reserve system can pass into both retail and wholesale inventory systems as the means of withdrawing and pushing equipment/materiel to the Marine forces in the operation area. The objective of the Marine Corps War Reserve Program is to ensure that acceptable levels of materiel are available to support the Marine forces during crisis or contingency operations. The War Reserve System interfaces with other Service's inventory systems including the DLA.

Joint Deployment Systems

Global Command and Control System

The global command and control system (GCCS) is the joint standard for command and control systems and is the communications and computer architecture for all joint systems to operate on. It supports the JOPES.

Time-Phased Force Deployment Data

The TPFDD registers all strategic (intertheater) sea and air movement requirements for deployment. The TPFDD is a part of GCCS and is an automated support tool for JOPES procedures.

Joint Flow and Analysis System for Transportation

Joint flow and analysis system for transportation (JFAST) is an analytical tool for estimating time and resources required to transport military forces under various scenarios and situations. It can analyze transportation requirements from point of origin to the POD.

Logistics Sustainment Analysis and Feasibility Estimator

Logistics sustainment analysis and feasibility estimator (LOGSAFE) aids the planner by assessing the sustainment feasibility of a proposed operations plan.

Global Transportation Network

The Global Transportation Network (GTN) is an automated transportation management system being developed as the vehicle for developing and maintaining ITV and total asset visibility.

Consolidated Aerial Ports System II

Consolidated aerial ports system II (CAPS II) provides an automated tool for AMC aerial ports with an automated C2 capability and the ability to process cargo and passenger movements.

Global Decision Support System

The global decision support system (GDSS) is an AMC system that schedules, tracks, and controls all air movements.

World Port System

The Worldwide Port System (WPS) supports the management, tracking, and documentation of U.S. cargo moving via ocean transportation.

CHAPTER 4. LANDING SUPPORT OPERATIONS

The Planning Process

An amphibious operation is characterized by the rapid build up of combat power ashore. A critical part of the amphibious operation is the planning and execution of landing the landing force. The LFSP provides the initial CSS to the landing force. The operations, intelligence, and CSS staff sections of the amphibious force focus LFSP planning and operations. The structure of the LFSP is based on the landing force's CSS requirements ashore. The LFSP's structure is determined during the planning phases of an amphibious operation.

The LFSP is formed and equipped to facilitate the landing and movement of personnel, supplies, and equipment across the beach, into HLZ or through a port; to evacuate casualties and EPWs; and to perform the beaching, retraction, and salvage of landing ships and crafts. The LFSP also must provide personnel and equipment to support the landing of airborne, air assault or helicopterborne forces, equipment, and supplies.

Preliminary Planning

The landing force's planning guidance comes from the amphibious operation's initiating directive. The CLF determines the extent of participation by unit commanders during preliminary planning. During preliminary planning, the CATF and CLF are responsible for the following:

- The CLF, with the concurrence of the CATF, selects primary and alternate landing areas.

- The CLF selects the landing beach and HLZs from information provided by the CATF.

- The CATF selects the tentative date and hour of landing after consultation with the CLF.

- The CLF develops the landing force concept of operations ashore. The CLF and CATF's decisions impact the CSSE and LFSP commanders' planning processes. Therefore, early and continuous

dissemination of planning data is essential to the CSSE and LFSP commanders.

Concurrent Planning

The CLF and the landing force staff maintain continuous liaison with subordinate commands to ensure understanding. One factor of particular concern to the LFSP is the determination of landing areas. The CLF selects landing areas that, consistent with the ability of surface and air units to provide support, will facilitate accomplishment of the landing force mission. It is essential that concurrent planning occurs between the landing force staff and subordinate commanders since time constraints can reduce planning opportunities. If possible, subordinate CSS planners should be included in operational planning.

Detailed Planning

The MAGTF, after coordination with landing force units, determines landing support assistance requirements. Based on these estimated requirements, the CSSE commander, LFSP commander, and LFSP staff request additional Marine Corps CSS units and equipment and/or Navy augmentation if required. The CSSE staff coordinates landing support planning with the appropriate staff section within the amphibious force.

Parallel Planning

Parallel planning is the continuous planning performed by the CATF and CLFs subordinate units and staffs to facilitate the execution of an amphibious landing. This coordination facilitates smooth landing operations.

Augmentation

The LFSP commander determines augmentation required from Marine Corps units or the Navy. The LFSP notifies the CSSE commander or the applicable staff officer. Requests for Navy augmentation must be made as early as possible during the planning process.

——————————————————————————————————————— MCWP 4-11.3

Planning Considerations

Principal considerations that affect the landing support mission and ultimately the structure of the LFSP include—

- Early, detailed analysis of the objective area.
- Analysis of tactical plans and their landing support requirements.
- Timely and complete training of the task-organized LFSP.
- Detailed planning for organization of BSAs and LZSA.
- Combat loading of each assault ship.
- Employment of the sea echelon concept.
- Establishment of adequate communications between tactical units, control elements, and landing support units (includes shore party and helicopter support).
- Defense requirements of BSAs and landing areas.
- Composition of the assault echelon and assault follow-on echelon.
- Evaluation of enemy activity and installations in the objective area.
- Establishment of the landing force's scheme of maneuver and landing plan.
- Evaluation of beach hydrographic conditions and terrain features inland from the beaches. This also includes HLZs.
- Quantity and types of supplies to be landed from assault shipping.
- Availability of personnel, supplies, and equipment for shore party operations.
- Availability of assault shipping.
- Development of plans for handling EPWs.
- Development of casualty evacuation and disaster recovery plans.
- Identification of coordination requirements with other agencies.
- Concept of CSS.

Planning Documents

Activation Order

The LFSP activation order is issued by the CLF. The LFSP activates on order of the CLF and is normally

terminated once the CSSE commander assumes responsibility for CSS ashore.

Note: The task organization of the shore party team/ group and HST creates units that require extensive training prior to landing support operations. Therefore, shore party teams/groups and HSTs must be activated as early as possible to allow organization and training prior to embarkation. The CLF is responsible for the control and coordination of these units.

Landing Force Support Party Operation Plan

The LFSP operation plan provides information and instructions required by the shore party or HST commanders to implement the CLFs decisions and concept of operations for a specific mission. It is normally published as a tab to appendix 14 to annex C.

Landing Force Support Party Appendix

The LFSP tab appendix 14 to annex C sets forth the concept of operations and the detailed and special tasks required to accomplish specific landing support missions. It contains control instructions and floating dump instructions, identifies pre-positioned emergency supplies, establishes priorities for LFSP equipment, and identifies missions assigned to each major subordinate section. It also identifies the relationship of landing support operations to the overall CSS and landing force schemes of maneuver.

Landing Force Support Party Order

The LFSP commander issues amplifying instructions to subordinates in the form of an operation order. These instructions only pertain to subordinate units and are, therefore, not suitable for inclusion in the LFSP tab to appendix 14 to annex C (Operations). If a complete LFSP order is used, the LFSP tab to appendix 14 to annex C (Operations) can be very brief. If the LFSP order is not detailed, the LFSP tab appendix 14 to annex C (Operations) must provide all necessary information.

Intelligence Considerations

Accurate and timely intelligence is the keystone to planning and decisionmaking. Once intelligence requirements are determined, all available information is studied and evaluated to prepare for the landing support mission. To plan landing support requirements effectively, the CLF requires detailed intelligence. Intelligence information must address—

- Topography.

- Local resources.

- Manmade obstructions.

- Climate.

- Routes of communications.

- Enemy methods.

- Enemy installations.

- Equipment and activities.

- Beaches.

- Hydrographic conditions (critical).

- Terrain immediately inland from the beaches and around landing zones.

- General character of surf and inshore currents and their effect on landing craft.

- Beach gradient and its affect on the beaching of landing craft and use of vehicles.

- Depth of water inshore, as related to determination of anchorage and maneuverability of supporting vessels.

- Composition of the beach and its influence on beaching and retracting landing craft and soil trafficability for personnel and vehicles.

- Tidal range of the designated beaches in relation to existing and reinforcing obstacles and beach widths.

- Location of obstacles as related to their influence on beaching landing craft or landing helicopters and debarking personnel and material.

- Range and time of tides.

Ship-to-Shore Movement

Ship-to-shore movement is that portion of an amphibious operation that moves the landing force off assault shipping and into a designated area. Its objective is to ensure the landing of troops, equipment, and supplies at the prescribed time and place. The LFSP is a temporary, task organization of the amphibious force that facilitates the landing and movement of troops, equipment, and supplies across beaches and into landing zones, ports, and airfields; assists in evacuating casualties and EPWs from beaches and landing zones; and assists in the beaching, retracting, and salvaging of landing ships and crafts. The CATF has overall responsibility for preparation of plans and control of the ship-to-shore movement. The CLF is responsible for determining the landing force's requirements for ship-to-shore movement. The responsibility for embarkation and landing of the LFSP rests with the supported tactical unit.

The landing support units are attached to the supported tactical unit for embarkation and landing purposes only. The type of control exercised in the ship-to-shore movement is based on the type of movement required and the concept of operations ashore. Typically, centralized control is exercised up to the limits of communications. The control system must provide for rapid fulfillment of landing force requirements ashore. The LFSP relies on three agencies afloat for the proper and timely execution of its mission: the Navy control group, helicopter logistics support center, and TACLOG. Detailed planning of the ship-to-shore movement begins after the landing forces' scheme of maneuver is determined and allocation of resources is finalized.

Final ship-to-shore planning is expressed in the landing plan. The landing plan establishes the landing priority among various elements of the landing force, provides overall coordination of ship-to-shore movement, and allocates resources. It is issued as tab C (Landing Plan) to appendix 14 (Amphibious Operations) to annex C (Operations).

See JPs 3-02.1 and 3-02.2 and FMFM 1-8 for detailed information.

Shore Party Team

There may be one or more shore party teams. The exact number of teams is contingent upon the landing plan. To support the assigned BSA effectively, the entire shore party team must be embarked aboard the same amphibious shipping so all elements of the team arrive at their destination at approximately the same time.

Normally, shore party teams land and establish designated beaches to support a unit the size of a BLT. Therefore, the shore party team's advance party is one of the first sections to land on the beach. The shore party team's remaining personnel and equipment are landed in an on-call wave as soon as the tactical situation allows.

Advance Party

The shore party team's advance party, embarked in two or more amphibious landing craft, lands as early as possible in the scheduled waves. Typically, the advance party consists of a command section, liaison section, communications section, and beach party section. The shore party and beach party team commanders land with the advance party. The advance party's liaison personnel and the landing force command echelon generally embark and land together.

Shore Platoon

The shore platoon is located near the line of departure at H-hour waiting for the order to land. The platoon is normally in a landing craft with pre-selected, high priority equipment from the motor transport/heavy equipment platoon. The shore platoon constructs beach exits and lateral roads, assists in the unloading of cargo and equipment from landing craft and landing ships, and helps the beach party team as required.

Service Platoon

The service platoon lands as directed by the shore party team and provides support to the team.

Motor Transport/Heavy Equipment Platoon

This platoon lands when the beach is secure enough to move heavy equipment ashore. It provides equipment to support the transportation needs of the shore party team. Therefore, motor transport/heavy equipment items not needed immediately by shore and service platoons are loaded into landing craft and called ashore as needed on nonscheduled waves.

Headquarters

The shore party team headquarters lands in an on-call wave and is phased ashore with other sections once the beach is organized and ready for the headquarters to take control. It does not land with the advance party.

Helicopter Support Team

HSTs land early in the ship-to-shore movement and establish landing zones that support a BLT-sized unit. The HST, like the shore party team, is a basic building block for the LFSP.

Shore Party Group

The shore party group consists of a headquarters, shore party team(s), and, if necessary, special attachments. Each group phases ashore as required.

The group headquarters lands once designated beaches are established, and they consolidate the existing shore party teams into the shore party group. It is embarked with the unit it supports. The command and communications sections embark on the same ship as the landing force commander. Before H-hour, the command and communications sections transfer with the TACLOG to the primary control vessel stationed off their assigned beach so they can monitor the landing of the shore party teams. Other sections, such as the military police and the motor transport and equipment section may be embarked on other ships in the embarkation group. The remainder of the shore party group headquarters, under command of the shore party group executive officer, should be embarked with the motor transport and equipment section.

The command section normally lands in two echelons: one echelon lands with the shore party group commander, and the other echelon lands with the shore party group executive officer. The shore party group commander and selected personnel are landed from a free boat as soon as consolidation and control of the shore party group can be effected. Remaining sections of the shore party group headquarters are in on-call or nonscheduled waves and land on request of the shore party group commander. Personnel in the replacement pool are landed as a first priority.

Beach Party Team

The Navy's beach party team usually lands in four echelons, three of which land in scheduled waves. The first echelon to land contains the beach party team's command echelon, and it lands with the shore party team's advance party. The second echelon lands in the same amphibious vehicle that contains the beach party team's command post equipment. This allows the beach party team commander to establish communications with Navy forces afloat and with adjacent beach party teams. The third echelon lands with the salvage section. The fourth echelon lands in an on-call wave with the rest of the shore party team. Refer to FMFM 1-8 for more information.

Landing Force Support Party

Once directed by the CLF, the LFSP commander moves the LFSP command post ashore to coordinate and consolidate the CSS efforts of the existing shore party teams/groups and to monitor and support the logistics activities of the HSTs, beach party group, and special attachments. The LFSP headquarters is formed when more than one shore party group or HST is included in the landing force.

Typically, the LFSP's command group is embarked with the landing force command group. The command group typically includes the LFSP commander, beach party commander, communications officer, manpower or personnel officer (G-1/S-1), G-3/S-3, and other selected staff assistants. The LFSP executive officer, G-4/S-4, and certain administrative personnel are normally embarked with the alternate landing force command group. Normally, the headquarters commandant is embarked with the LFSP headquarters' remaining personnel and equipment. Special attachments to the LFSP are embarked in available shipping in accordance with the landing plan.

Prior to H-hour, the LFSP commander, advance command group, and the TACLOG transfer to the control vessel. The LFSP commander and command group land in an on-call wave. The LFSP commander

may land in a nonscheduled wave if he is required earlier or later than anticipated. The executive officer and alternate command group land in a free boat separate from the LFSP commander. The remainder of the LFSP lands as requested by the LFSP commander.

Operations Ashore

Landing support operations begin with the landing of the advance parties and continue until the landing support operation is completed or relieved. The LFSP remains functional until the landing support operation is terminated or the CSSE commander relieves the LFSP of its responsibilities. The primary CSS beach is designated during the planning stage and will be known as the BSA. The BSA remains operational and is the primary means of support to the landing force during subsequent operations ashore.

Shore Party Team

Shore party team operations vary based on the landing plan and scheme of maneuver. The shore party team's advance party reconnoiters the beach and road net and verifies proposed sites for beach installations. The command section marks the beach center and flanks and then begins development of the BSA. Once the entire shore party team has landed, they—

- Organize the BSA.
- Establish basic communications capabilities.
- Locate dumps inland.
- Establish facilities for limited equipment repair.
- Establish evacuation stations.

The shore party team's goal is to prepare and maintain beaching points and access roads, move troops and equipment across the beach rapidly, and reduce/avoid congestion on the beach. The shore party team unloads, segregates, stores, safeguards, and issues supplies as they are brought ashore. Support operations are decentralized and the primary source for combat service support is still the tactical units located aboard ship. Only those service support units that operate in direct support of the combat units are landed early.

Minimum preplanned levels of supply are established ashore once the tactical situation begins to develop and additional shore party equipment, personnel, and supplies have landed. Shore party team operations are then centralized under a shore party group. Consolidated control usually does not involve physical consolidation of combat service support installations.

Operations of the combat service support sections in the BSA are directed by the shore party team commander, who allocates areas to all units in the BSA and coordinates local defense and security. The shore party team organizes the BSA and develops inland supply facilities into combat service support areas.

Advance Party

The advance party of the shore party team is the first shore party section to land. The advance party reconnoiters the beach and road net and verifies tentatively selected sites for beach installations. The advance party's command section marks the beach center and flanks and begins development of the BSA in preparation for the landing of follow-on troops. If possible, beaches are established in close proximity to each other to ease consolidation once the shore party group lands. The advance party establishes the advance command post and erects flank and center markers that indicate the limits of the beach for which they have primary responsibility. The beach party team commander and staff establish their command post close to the shore party team's command post. They then erect range markers and other navigational devices as required. After the beach organization is accomplished, personnel reconnoiter dump routes and locations for future beach combat service support installations.

Shore Platoon

The shore platoon constructs beach exits and lateral roads and assists in the unloading of cargo and equipment from landing crafts and ships. They also assist the beach party team as required.

Service Platoon

Service platoon personnel compose the initial supply/ammunition dump sections. They establish dump areas and organize the beach in depth. Facilities in the dump

are further developed as additional personnel arrive. Operations in the BSA and in the dumps vary in every operation. Therefore, unit assignments and specific jobs to be performed should be clearly delineated in the LFSP operation order.

Motor Transport/Heavy Equipment Platoon

The motor transport/heavy equipment platoon provides equipment to support the shore party team's transportation needs. Once the shore party team is firmly established ashore, all equipment and motor transport operations revert to the control of the motor transport/heavy equipment platoon commander.

Headquarters

Once ashore, the headquarters' command section takes control of the advance command post and completes the command and control facilities. The organization, location, and function of the shore party team command post depend on whether the team is operating independently or as part of a shore party group. If operating independently, it may approach the size and complexity of a group command post. If operating as part of a shore party group, the group normally assumes the functions performed by the shore party team command post. The team headquarters establishes, in the center of the beach, an information center/clearing station. This center/clearing station assists personnel crossing the beach locate their parent units. It is operated by the shore party team until it is relieved by the shore party group.

- **Security Section.** The security section organizes its sector of defense within the BSA. If the team is operating independently, it organizes the defense of the entire BSA. If adjacent to another team, it coordinates its sector of defense with the adjacent team's and the shore party group commander's. The security section provides the ground defense weapons organic to the landing support platoon, assigns defense positions, and organizes various other sections of the shore party team for defense.

- **Communications Section.** The communications section establishes local communications for internal control. If supporting an assault BLT, the communications section must establish communications with the headquarters of the supported BLT, the TACLOG serving the BLT, and the parent shore party group. See MCWP 6-22 for more information.

- **Evacuation Section.** The evacuation section is located near the center of the beach and prepares for receipt and evacuation of casualties. These facilities are austere, but they must be prepared to hold casualties if evacuation is not immediate. Facilities must protect casualties from the elements and enemy action. Medical treatment is limited to emergency measures only.

- **MP Section.** The MP section deploys to assigned traffic control points and establishes control in the BSA. They also establish an EPW collection point and evacuate or hold EPWs. The MP section also establishes straggler collection points for personnel separated from their units.

Shore Party Group

After the shore party group lands, the shore party group commander coordinates the consolidation of existing shore party teams into the shore party group. The shore party group commander is directly responsible to the LFSP commander for organization, operation, and defense of the BSA. The landing plan and scheme of maneuver determine the shore party group's operations. The organization and disposition of the shore party teams and the size of the landing force determine if the shore party group operates two or more BSAs.

The shore party group headquarters is organized around the headquarters section of a landing support company, TSB, and augmented as required. Immediately upon landing, the shore party group headquarters is established with one of the shore party teams on the beach. This allows the shore party group commander to supervise operations of the shore party teams.

Command Section

The command section commands, controls, and coordinates the efforts of the shore party teams, as they are absorbed into the shore party group. This section is responsible for the administrative needs of the shore party group and maintains up-to-date supply records. If appropriate, this section consolidates shore

party team security sections into a group security section to provide defense for the BSA.

MP Section

The MP section is assigned local defense and security missions and supervises the operations of the MPs assigned to the shore party teams.

Evacuation Section

The evacuation section is located near the shore party group's command post. It maintains records and plans for casualty evacuation from the BSA and provides medical care for the shore party group headquarters.

Communications Section

The communications section expands existing capabilities as required to meet the needs of the shore party group.

Motor Transport and Equipment Section

The motor transport and equipment section records the status and operational assignment of all attached equipment and motor transport items.

Replacement Pool

Replacement personnel are generally placed in defensive positions in the BSA or assigned to dump areas as required. Replacement officers are assigned duties in shore party teams and shore party group task organizations until they are needed as replacements in the tactical units.

Beach Party Team Headquarters

This section is established near the shore party group's command post. Once the beach party group establishes communications with the beach party teams, it assumes control of beach party team operations.

Helicopter Support Team

The HST provides terminal guidance to helicopters landing in the HLZ they also provide rigging and external lift equipment and supplies to forward areas of operation. These teams are responsible for their own security.

Landing Force Support Party

Once ashore, the LFSP commander assumes control of landing support operations. The LFSP organizes a main command post. Shore party groups and HSTs are not consolidated into the LFSP main command post. The shore party group serves as the alternate command post. It is located separately in the BSA. The LFSP's main command post coordinates and assists the shore party groups and HSTs, and its functions vary only slightly from that of the shore party group's command post.

The shore party group commander is ashore and operating in the BSA prior to the arrival of the LFSP headquarters. Therefore, the LFSP headquarters establishes itself ashore as soon as possible and usually locates itself within the BSA of the major combat service support effort. The following sections make up the LFSP headquarters:

Command and Administrative Section. The command section is responsible for the command and control and administrative (e.g., messing, billeting) functions of the LFSP. This section maintains records on dump status, ships' unloading status, location of ships, serials requested and landed, beach/landing force developments, tactical situation, casualty and EPW evacuations, and other data as directed. It consolidates and forwards reports from the shore party groups and HSTs to the appropriate headquarters. Requests for other than routine supply requirements are received and handled by this section.

Medical Section. The medical section plans the LFSP's medical evacuation functions, supervises patient operations, and prepares medical evacuation reports. In addition, this section provides medical services for personnel located in the immediate vicinity of the LFSP headquarters.

MP Section. This section supervises the shore party and HST's MP sections. It also establishes the landing force's EPW stockades and organizes and evacuates EPWs from the objective area.

Communications Section. The communications section expands existing capabilities as required to meet the needs of the LFSP.

Motor Transport and Equipment Section. This section provides the transportation and equipment requirements needed by the LFSP headquarters.

Liaison Section. This section consists of personnel attached or under the operational control of the LFSP. The critical function of liaison personnel are to monitor, coordinate, advise, and assist the LFSP in its dealings with their parent unit.

Organization of the Beach

Different emphasis is placed on beaches within the amphibious objective area at different times. Prior planning determines control of the primary combat service support beach. The CSS beach remains in operation and is the primary means of support to the landing force during operations ashore. Therefore, it must be organized effectively to accomplish assigned shore party tasks and efficiently unload both single and mixed categories of equipment and supplies. Based on the tactical situation, beaches are organized to receive classes of supplies under several conditions. The organization of the beach is planned prior to the landing of the LFSP commander or designated representatives. After landing, the LFSP commander may adjust the beach's organization if required.

Designated Beach

A designated beach, represented by a color, is generally the responsibility of a shore party group. Each shore party team handles two of the following types of supplies: fuel, rations, miscellaneous supplies, ammunition. Separate facilities for unloading supplies delivered by tracked and wheeled vehicles and evacuation of casualties are provided. However, if the tactical scheme of maneuver requires that beaches be separated, each shore party team is responsible for the preparation of their assigned beach. The shore party group headquarters lands on the designated beach scheduled to handle the major combat service support effort. This beach and the area to its rear are developed into a BSA. Other beach operations are abandoned once sufficient means are established to support the landing force. The shore party team and its equipment are then displaced to the main unloading point for throughput operations.

Numbered Beach

A numbered beach is the responsibility of a shore party team. If the tactical scheme calls for the landing force to land in columns of battalions, a shore party team is embarked with each leading battalion. The first team to land organizes installations ashore to support the landing BLT and subsequent BLTs landing in column. The shore party team in support of the BLT landing abreast assumes the responsibility for half the basic colored beach and supports the landing of the next column of BLTs. This would result in colored beach 1 and colored beach 2. The shore party group headquarters lands immediately behind the first shore party team so that it can coordinate the efforts of both teams when the second team comes ashore. Normally, shore party teams land and establish numbered beaches. If possible, numbered beaches are established close to each other to allow consolidation of two or more under a shore party group. If numbered beaches are separated by distances that prevent control by the same primary control ship (regardless of the size of the landing force or the length of the beach front), they assume the control of the designated beach for the landing.

Types of Unloading Points

Individual unloading points are established based on the type of supplies handled. They are normally categorized as follows.

Fuel. During the assault, Classes III(A) and III(W) fuels are taken ashore in bladders, drums, and refuelers. The unloading point marker is located near an existing or recently constructed roadway that leads off the beach to an area suitable for fuel container storage. Also, the use of a ship-to-shore pipe system may be necessary for an alternate or additional fuel point located on the flank of the beach. Its location must not interfere with unloading.

Rations. Rations are unloaded either by pallets, ISO containers or cargo net. Therefore, the unloading point must have hard surface areas to accommodate forklifts or rough terrain MHE. Storage areas for pallets, containers, and cargo nets also need to be established.

Miscellaneous Supplies. Miscellaneous supplies constitute all classes of supplies, except fuel, rations or ammunition that are not carried ashore by troops. These supplies are packed in varying configurations and the unloading points must be able to accommodate pallets, special slings, and MHE.

Ammunition. The ammunition unloading point's organization is similar to the fuel unloading point. Hard surfaced areas and road systems are required. The unloading point must be located a safe distance from the BSA and the fuel unloading point. A special ammunition supply point also will need to be established.

Tracked Vehicles. Tracked vehicles unload their cargo at predesignated points on the beach. These points and access lanes are cleared and marked by engineer or mine clearance personnel. Combat engineer signs (dated and signed by the person that cleared the area) mark cleared areas of the beach.

Wheeled Vehicles. The landing of wheeled vehicles requires special preparations. Roadways need to be cleared of mines, leveled, and beach mobility matting (MOMAT) laid. Vehicles are parked in an assembly area until their parent unit needs them. Combat engineers mark cleared areas of the beach.

Mixed Categories of Equipment and Supplies

Causeways are used where landing craft cannot reach the beach or where they will facilitate the movement of supplies and equipment to the beach. If causeways are used, the organization of the beach is as follows:

- Shore party's advance party erects flank and center markers to mark beach limits.

- Shore party's advance party erects range markers to indicate where causeways beach.

- Amphibious construction battalion personnel place and operate the causeways and control all operations within the causeways.

- Shore party is responsible for construction, maintenance, and traffic control of the roadway leading from the causeway inland.

Appendix A contains a listing of standard beach and landing site markers. No other unloading point markers are used on the beach unless landing craft also use the beach. Traffic is directed without interruption to the inland combat service support areas or to the GCE. Casualties are evacuated directly to designated casualty receiving and treatment ships. EPWs are evacuated to EPW receiving ships. If causeways are not used, the beach party erects range markers and the landing force component of the shore party prepares ramp approaches. Evacuation of casualties and EPWs is executed as stated above.

Organization and Operation of the Beach Support Area

Organization of the BSA facilitates the receiving and distributing of supply classes needed during the initial phases of the landing. The BSA must be organized to handle EPWs, casualties, helicopters, wheeled vehicles, and lost personnel. To facilitate rapid unloading, initial supplies and equipment should be vehicle-loaded, palletized or in packaged lifts and stowed in assault shipping to permit rapid transfer to amphibious vehicles, landing craft, trucks or helicopters. This reduces congestion at the water's edge and allows supplies to be moved rapidly inland to using units or separate inland dumps. The following criteria affect the location and organization of the BSA. Figure 4-1 contains a suggested layout for a BSA.

- Supply sections should be located in sites that provide the best dispersion, cover and concealment, and availability of existing lines of communications.

- Internal arrangement of the BSA must provide for maximum traffic circulation.

- Supplies located within the dumps are segregated by type or other distinguishing characteristics to ensure rapid inventory and issue.

- Manpower requirements are reduced if mechanical equipment is used to handle cargo.

- Fuel and ammunition must be separated and dug-in or revetted (use dozers to accomplish this work rapidly).

- Floodlight trailers and fire-fighting equipment are located within the dump area.

- HLZs, properly marked and equipped with wind direction markers and other essential control or navigational aids, are established near each supply dump, shore party command post, and casualty evacuation point.

In addition to the supply sections, other combat service support functions exist in the BSA.

Amphibious Assault Fuel System. The landing force requires tremendous amounts of Classes III(A) and III(W) fuels. To facilitate the early landing of the landing force, bulk fuel units are attached to the shore party team. The shore party team makes provisions for adequate space, administrative support, and protection for these units within the BSA. These units prepare for bulk delivery of Class III(A) and III(W) fuels using the amphibious assault fuel system (AAFS). AAFS equipment is mobile-loaded on vehicles and landed early in the operation. Additional information on the AAFS is provided in MCWP 3-17, *Engineer Operations*.

Aviation Support. The shore party team is responsible for the support of aviation units landed from assault shipping. Aviation technical personnel, equipped with special cargo handling equipment, are attached to the shore party team during the landing and establishment of the BSA. The shore party team establishes dumps for aviation peculiar Class II, III(A), IV, and V(A) supplies that cannot be moved directly to air installations. Provisions to repair, refuel,

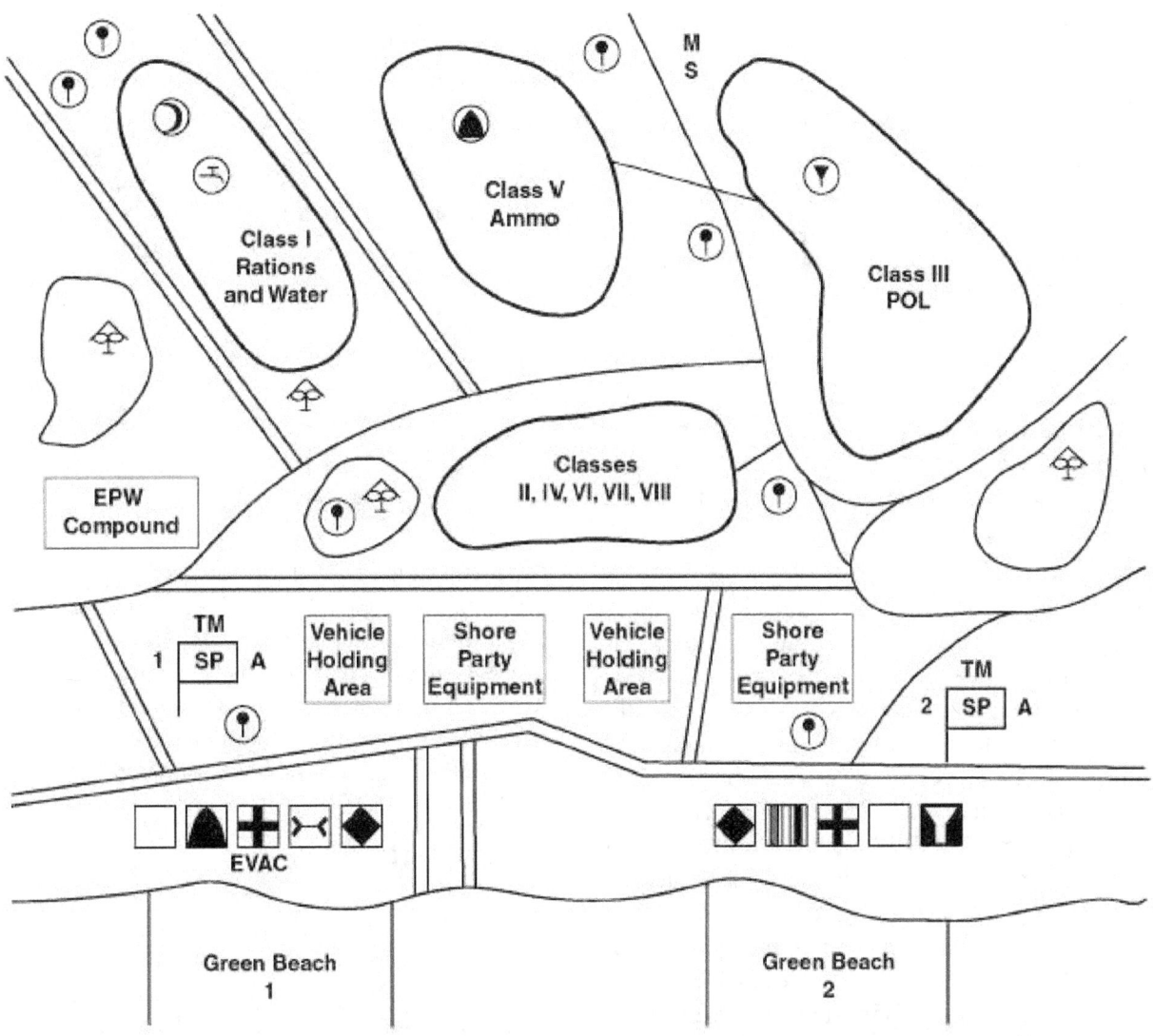

Figure 4-1. General Layout of BSA.

and rearm helicopters and vertical takeoff and landing aircraft may also be required.

Vehicle Parking and Repair. The large number of vehicles landed in support of the landing force requires a vehicle parking and maintenance area that is established by specialists attached to the shore party team from sections of the CSSE. This area is removed from the beach area and located within the shore party's defensive scheme.

Troop Assembly Areas. Reserve and support troops are quickly moved off the beach and into predesignated assembly areas to facilitate their employment in landing force operations and to reduce congestion of the beach.

Their time in the assembly area may vary from a few hours to several days. The shore party team orients these units as to the tactical situation and assimilates them into the BSA defense plan. While units are in the assembly areas, the shore party provides them with any required combat service support.

Water Supply Points

Water supply points should be within the BSA so that the shore party team can provide for their defensive and administrative support. Their locations are predetermined and their establishment and exact locations are reported to higher headquarters.

Casualty Evacuation

Evacuation of casualties from the BSA is a function of the LFSP. Evacuation station personnel land with the shore party team and HST headquarters, establish beach evacuation stations on each shore party team beach and HST landing zone, and assume evacuation responsibility. As the assault progresses, evacuation stations and personnel may be consolidated into the shore party group, HST or LFSP. This allows movement of casualties and makes maximum effective use of landing craft and helicopters. Basic evacuation procedures continue in effect after consolidation. The number of casualties treated ashore increase as more elaborate medical facilities are established ashore.

Medical Regulating Team. Casualties not taken directly by helicopter to medical facilities afloat are evacuated to the beach evacuation station. Those requiring immediate evacuation are sent from the beach evacuation station by the most expeditious means available. Waterborne casualty-carrying craft report initially to the primary control ship. A medical regulating team (MRT) is located on the primary control ship or casualty receiving and treatment ship. The MRT provides destination information to waterborne casualty-carrying craft. Casualties also can be evacuated directly from the beach evacuation station to casualty receiving and treatment ships equipped with helicopter platforms or to hospital ships if available. The destination of the helicopterborne casualties is controlled by the helicopter direction center and assisted by an MRT representative. Detailed information on the evacuation of casualties is provided in MCWP 4-11.1, *Health Services Support Operations*.

Evacuation Stations. The primary role of an evacuation station is to facilitate the evacuation of assault force casualties to a designated casualty receiving and treatment ship. The LFSP-established evacuation stations are formed from assets of the medical battalion. During the initial assault stage, medical personnel from the battalion aid station may be required to establish an evacuation station until the shore party is ashore. The buildup of health service support facilities ashore continues as the tactical

situation permits. The initial facility establishes shore-based capabilities for emergency surgery. The LFSP commander and the landing force surgeon determine the location of the evacuation station. They are generally located in an area with good approach roads and protection that will facilitate patient care while they await evacuation. An HLZ is prepared in the same area. Refer to MCWP 4-11.1 for further details.

Note: Plans for evacuation of casualties also include provisions for property exchange of critical items, such as litters, blankets, splints, and certain other medical equipment.

EPW and Civilian Enclosures

Elements of the LFSP locate and construct civilian and EPW enclosures. EPW and civilian enclosures are separated from each other and from other combat service support installations. They are located within the BSA's defense system and must be of sufficient size to provide for the detainees' physical needs. Medical support is provided as required.

EPW Collection Points

Typically, the shore party team commander establishes EPW collection points in or near the landing beaches. HSTs also establish collection points in HLZs. Collection points are indicated on the combat service support overlay. If a large number of EPWs are anticipated early in the assault, ships are designated to receive and evacuate EPWs.

Units that capture EPWs are responsible for delivering them to EPW collection points. MPs assume control of the EPWs once they are delivered to the collection points. EPWs are either retained at the collection points or evacuated to an EPW ship. The shore party group ensures that—

- Collection points are established on the beach and landing zones and the intelligence officer of the highest headquarters is notified of their location.

- Personnel are designated to construct temporary EPW enclosures.

- An adequate number of guards are available.

- The collection, evacuation, and safeguarding of EPWs are coordinated with the appropriate unit.

- Control of EPW facilities is relinquished as directed. This is normally done when the MP unit is ashore and functioning.

Salvage Operations

Shore party salvage operations can be divided into two categories—

- Salvage of landing craft, amphibious vehicles, and landing force equipment damaged during the landing.

- Salvage of landing force equipment damaged or rendered inoperable during the conduct of operations ashore.

The NBG salvages landing craft and vehicles that broach at the waters edge. Amphibious vehicles, trucks or other landing force vehicles damaged or sunk in the vicinity of the beach are salvaged by the beach party and then moved to maintenance and repair facilities. Salvage collection points are established in the BSA by maintenance units. Mobile maintenance and repair teams can frequently affect salvage of collected equipment without evacuating vehicles or pieces of equipment. Salvaged articles reduce the amount of necessary resupply and replacement for the landing force.

CHAPTER 5. OTHER TRANSPORTATION SUPPORT OPERATIONS

Air Movement Operations

Air movement operations require detailed planning and preparation by the deploying unit. The MAGTF embarkation officer handles the planning and preparations required for the air movement. Air movement operations involve marshalling transported units into the staging area; loading supplies, equipment, and personnel at the departure airfield; and receiving/dispersing supplies, equipment, and personnel at the arrival airfield. An air movement operation consists of two phases: the planning and preparation phase, and the execution phase.

The DACG and the AACG are an integral part of the airfield's organization. The DACG and AACG's missions are to provide the personnel and equipment required to coordinate, inspect, direct, and assist the deploying units' move through aerial ports of embarkation or debarkation. The deploying unit and the USAF TALCE comprise the remaining major organizations at the airfield. Additional units, civilian agencies or contracted support may fall under the cognizance of the DACG/AACG or the TALCE. Close coordination between the DACG, AACG, TALCE, and the deploying unit(s) is essential to ensure smooth execution of air movement.

Organization

The DACG and AACG's organizations are mission dependent. The DACG is task-organized with personnel and equipment that will not accompany the deploying unit to the destination airfield. The AACG should be pre-positioned at the arrival airfield before unit movement begins. If advance deployment of the AACG is not possible, it should move to the arrival airfield with the lead elements of the transported unit.

The DACG and AACG's organizational structures should provide, at a minimum, the following capabilities:

- Command.
- Administration.
- Statistics.
- Operations.
- Logistics (i.e., maintenance, supply, and medical).
- Joint inspections.
- Load/unload teams.
- Communications.

The DACG and AACG are task-organized units that coordinate and direct the throughput of personnel, equipment, and supplies at the aerial port of embarkation/aerial port of debarkation. The beach and terminal operations company, TSB provides the nucleus for the DACG and AACG. The operations section of the beach and terminal operations company provides the nucleus for the control element of the DACG and AACG. The shipping and receiving platoon of the beach and terminal operations company provides the technical expertise required for traffic management (military occupational specialty 3112, Traffic Management Specialists). The TSB provides MHE support, communications support, and maintenance support. The FSSG provides additional communications support or security support if required.

Augmentation of personnel may be obtained from the longshoremen platoon of the beach and terminal operations company and the landing support companies. Additional personnel and equipment support also may be provided by organizations assigned to the airfield, civilian contractors or host nation support (if applicable).

Tasks and Responsibilities

Airfield operations and their accompanying tasks and responsibilities are normally subdivided into organizational zones of responsibility: departure airfield operations and arrival airfield operations. Departure airfield operations are subdivided into the marshalling area, alert holding area, call forward area, and loading ramp area. Arrival airfield operations are subdivided into the unloading ramp area, holding area, and unit area.

Deploying Unit

During deployment airfield operations, the deploying unit has the marshalling area as its unit zones of responsibility (see figure 5-1). The deploying unit prepares for air movement; assembles vehicles, equipment, supplies, and personnel into chalks (loads); delivers chalks to the alert holding area; and provides the required dunnage/shoring to accompany its loads. Its major functions include—

- Preparing personnel and cargo manifests.
- Preparing other documentation agreed upon during the joint planning conference.
- Conducting initial inspection of each chalk.
- Releasing chalks to the DACG at the alert holding area.

During arrival airfield operations, the deploying unit has the unit area as its zone of responsibility. It receives chalks from the AACG and terminates the air movement. The DACG has the alert holding area/call forward area as its zone of responsibility. The DACG ensures chalks are moved forward to the ready line and released to the TALCE in accordance with the established movement plan. Its major functions include—

- Accepting chalks from deploying unit.
- Conducting inspections.
- Establishing communications with deploying unit.
- Establishing functional areas and backup communications with TALCE.
- Assisting in joint inspection with the TALCE and/or the appropriate movement control agency.
- Establishing a joint inspection area (i.e., checkpoint 1) and a final briefing area/final manifest correction area (i.e., checkpoint 2).
- Establishing statistical data.

Appendix B contains a DACG checklist.

AACG

The AACG has the holding area as its zone of responsibility during arrival airfield operations (see figure 5-2). It receives and processes chalks for release to the deploying MAGTF. Its major functions include—

- Assembling chalks.
- Inspecting for completeness.
- Providing minor services (e.g., gas, oil, minor maintenance).
- Developing statistical data.

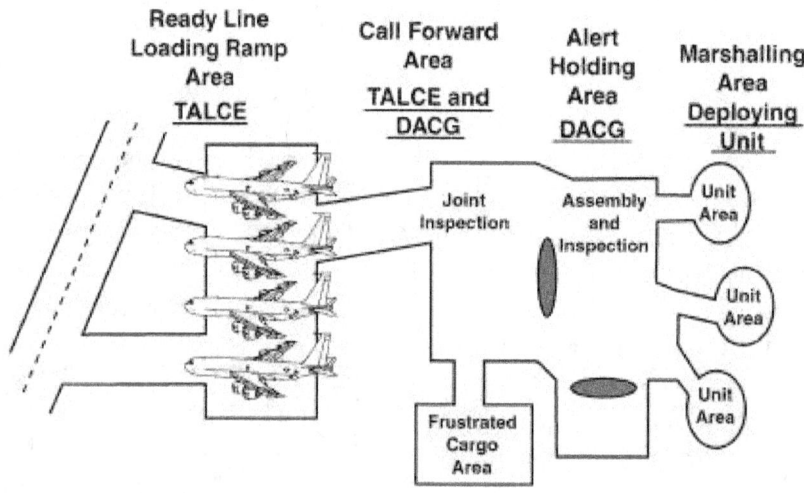

Figure 5-1. Departure Zones of Responsibility.

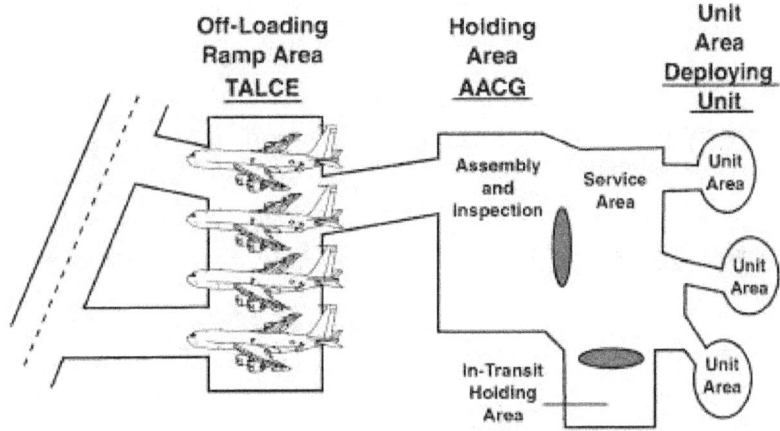

Figure 5-2. Arrival Airfield Areas of Responsibility.

- Establishing radio links to the unit area and functional area.

- Establishing backup communications in the unloading area with the TALCE.

- Establishing a temporary storage area.

Appendix C contains an AACG checklist.

Planning Considerations

See appendix D for a list of specific requirements during the planning and preparation phase.

Coordination Requirements

Air movement operations require close coordination with all participating units. The DACG and AACG coordinate with the TALCE and/or the appropriate movement control agency to ensure smooth operations. It is essential that the unit movement officers of the embarking units contact the DACG as early as possible. This allows the DACG to coordinate the arrival of the unit and gear to be staged for movement aboard an aircraft. The movement officers must coordinate with the AACG to coordinate receipt of gear and arrival of follow-on personnel and gear.

Execution

See appendix E for a list of specific requirements during the execution phase.

Air Delivery Operations

Air delivery is the in-flight delivery of specially rigged equipment and supplies to land-based combat forces. It is performed by either fixed-wing or rotary-wing aircraft. Air delivery is a combat service support sub-function and is normally coordinated by the CSSE. The CSSE commander determines if air delivery is the appropriate mode of transportation.

Organization

The Marine Corps' primary air delivery unit is the air delivery platoon of the TSB beach and terminal operations company. The air delivery platoon's mission is to receive, store, repair, and rig selected supplies and equipment for airdrop from either Marine or Air Force aircraft.

The air delivery platoon is organized into a 4-member headquarters section and 2 operating sections of 30 personnel each. TSB beach and terminal operations company provides the air delivery platoon with motor transport, communications, and MHE capabilities.

Tasks and Responsibilities

Supported Unit

The supported unit receives airdropped supplies and equipment. The supported unit's responsibilities include—

- Identifying the type and quantities of supplies required.

- Requesting resupply through appropriate channels.

- Selecting, marking, and operating drop zones.

- Recovering airdropped supplies and equipment from drop zones.

- Recovering, staging, safeguarding, and evacuating air delivery equipment (including parachutes) to the rigging site.

Air Delivery Platoon

The air delivery platoon's responsibilities include—

- Receiving, temporarily storing, and preparing supplies and equipment for airdrop.

- Performing organizational and intermediate maintenance on airdropped equipment (including parachutes and platforms).

- Ensuring equipment is inspected and certified as required.

- Providing supervision, technical assistance, and advice on the operation of drop zones and the recovery and evacuation of airdropped equipment from drop zones.

- Furnishing personnel to assist in the pre and post loading inspections of airdropped loads.

- Providing technical advice and assistance to other units involved in parachute operations if necessary.

- Assisting in loading supplies and equipment into aircraft.

- Providing auxiliary personnel to aid flight crews in performance of the airdrop mission if necessary.

CSSE

The CSSE's responsibilities include—

- Determining mode and method of resupply.

- Tasking the air delivery platoon with airdrop missions.

- Providing supplies and equipment for airdrop.

- Transporting supplies and/or equipment from storage areas (dumps) to the rigging site(s).

- Providing the support required by the air delivery platoon (i.e., MHE, motor transport, and communications).

- Requesting the airlift support required to accomplish the airdrop mission.

- Providing support to the air delivery platoon for replacement of airdrop equipment and consumables used in rigging.

- Acting as coordinator to ensure airdrop loads are marshaled and loaded aboard supporting aircraft (air delivery platoon may assist).

- Verifying receipt of supplies by supported unit.

Airlifting Unit

The airlifting unit is the aviation unit that provides the aircraft to accomplish the airdrop mission. Responsibilities of the airlifting unit differ slightly depending on whether Marine or Air Force assets are used. If Marine assets are used, the responsibility rests with the air delivery platoon to provide additional equipment and personnel. If Air Force assets are used, the responsibility to provide additional equipment and personnel rests with the Air Force. Airlifting units, regardless of Service affiliation, have the following responsibilities:

- Provide appropriate aircraft to accomplish the assigned mission and advise the supported unit on the method of delivery.

- Provide airdrop inspectors to conduct pre- and post-loading joint inspections with the air delivery platoon.

- Supervise the loading of the aircraft.

- Deliver the loads to the appropriate drop zones.

Planning Considerations

Generally, planning for air delivery operations is conducted by higher headquarters. The amount of airdrop support required is determined and the concept of operations is developed. The CSSE commander determines the mode of transportation required to support the requesting units. The strategic mobility or AMC liaison officer located in the G-4 identifies and tasks airlift assets based upon mission requirement. This may require liaison with external agencies such as the TALCE or mobile aerial port squadron (MAPS). The concept of employment is developed and air delivery assets are positioned to best support the assigned mission. The staging area, when supplies and equipment are to be airdropped, is collocated with the air delivery platoon along with supporting equipment and personnel. Air delivery support request procedures are developed and specific command and control procedures are established. Supported units are trained to operate drop zones and to recover/evacuate airdrop equipment. Once planning and training are accomplished, the air delivery operation moves to the execution phase.

Several considerations greatly impact the planning process of an air delivery operation—

- The air delivery platoon cannot support itself. Augmentation involves administrative support, liaison personnel, and transportation (i.e., MHE, communications, and motor transport).

- The supply support required to sustain the air delivery is extensive, for example, large amounts of expendable supplies (e.g., plywood) are required. The supported unit must provide this material.

- Airdrop operations require large numbers of skilled, highly trained personnel.

- The air delivery platoon's command and control procedures must be clearly defined. This is critical if the platoon is not deployed or collocated with its parent unit.

- The air delivery platoon is generally positioned at an airfield that can conduct fixed wing operations.

The following requirements also must be addressed during planning:

- Special requirements must be determined; e.g., the need to airdrop engineer equipment or other large platform loads.

- Adequate storage/operating facilities at or near the departure airfield. These facilities (hangers are preferred but tents will suffice) should protect airdrop equipment from adverse weather.

- Electrical power for lighting, sewing machines, tools, and fans used to repair and pack large cargo parachutes and airdrop equipment.

- Special sites may have to be established for rigging and storage of ammunition and POL airdrop loads.

- MHE may be required to move/load airdrop containers and platforms, also to move supplies during the rigging process.

- Prime movers and trailers may be required to move rigged loads from the rigging site to the aircraft.

- Close liaison must be established between the platoon and the airlifted unit to coordinate marshalling, loading, and inspection of airdrop loads.

- Communications support is required to coordinate rigging and loading activities.

Coordination Requirements

Air delivery operations require coordination between supported and supporting sections. The air delivery platoon locates, rigs, marshals, and assists in delivery of supplies and equipment in conjunction with the ACE, other air components, and the supporting aircraft. Detailed coordination with the G-3/S-3 and the fire control sections is required to ensure that air deliveries do not conflict with supporting fires or other air operations.

Execution

Typically, the air delivery platoon arrives in the area of operations with limited equipment and personnel. To provide effective support, the platoon and its higher headquarters must know in advance what airdrop support will be required; i.e., amount of supplies to be airdropped, aircraft availability, the threat, duration of the operation, and special requirements. The air delivery platoon performs the following functions:

- Establishes and operates airdrop rigging site.

- Advises the CSSE commander concerning method and type of airdrop to be used.

- Receives, stores, and rigs air-delivered equipment and supplies in accordance with appropriate procedures.

- Prepares rigged airdrop loads for movement to the aircraft.

- Participates in joint airdrop inspections for the pre-/post-loading inspections of air loads.

- Assists, as required, in the loading of airdrop loads aboard aircraft.

- Provides assistance in training supported units in the operation and marking of drop zones and the recovery of airdrop equipment and parachutes.

- Provides, as required, flight crew augmentation for Marine airdrop aircraft.

Helicopter Support Team Operations

The use of helicopterborne forces in the amphibious assault is one of the landing force's most important tactical weapons because it can project power ashore and exploit enemy weaknesses. However, the use of helicopterborne forces also requires detailed planning and integration at all levels of the amphibious force. Planning that supports helicopterborne units is generally complex and must support units in a rapidly changing environment. Confusion that disrupts the rapid buildup of combat power into the HLZ can be fatal. Therefore, a helicopterborne unit's CSS must be tailored to helicopterborne operations. The primary CSS organization for helicopterborne units is the HST. However, the helicopterborne unit commander is responsible for all aspects of the operation within the HLZ. The supported unit receives support and augmentation from other MAGTF organizations, but the helicopterborne unit commander retains operational control.

Role of the LFSP

The role of the LFSP in supporting a helicopterborne operation depends on the MAGTF's mission and task organization. The level of support provided to the helicopterborne unit by the LFSP may vary from training in landing zone operations to providing enough personnel and equipment to form the HST headquarters and landing zone platoon if a CSS buildup is required.

The LFSP controls, maintains, and manages the slings and cargo nets used for external helicopter lifts.

However, the helicopterborne unit and its attachments are responsible for preparing, rigging (attaching slings), and hooking (to the helicopter) their organic equipment and supplies for external helicopter lift. The HST provides training assistance in the use of this equipment to MAGTF units.

HST Tasks

The HST performs tasks within the landing zone similar to those performed by the shore party team/group in the BSA. An HST performs the following tasks:

- Prepares, maintains, and marks landing sites.

- Removes or marks obstacles.

- Erects wind direction indicators, (e.g., wind socks), panels, and range lights (used during night operations).

- Establishes and maintains the required communications. This includes communicating with supporting helicopters, Tailcoats, and the Navy control organization.

- Reconnoiters and selects areas for supply dumps and other combat service support installations, HST command post, casualty evacuation stations, and defensive positions that provide landing zone security.

- Directs and controls helicopter operations and support units within the landing zone.

- Unloads helicopters (including external lifts).

- Loads cargo nets, pallets, and slings on board helicopters.

- Loads EPWs and casualties on board helicopters.

- Establishes dumps.

- Issues supplies.

- Maintains supply records (i.e., supplies received, issued, and available).

- Maintains the helicopterborne unit's basic load at the prescribed level.

- Passes requests for replenishment (i.e., basic load, supplies not contained in the HLZ dumps, on-call serials) to the helicopterborne unit TACLOG that is collocated with the helicopter direction center.

- Provides personnel and vehicle ground control.

- Maintains a situation map and information center.

- Provides emergency helicopter repair and refueling as required.
- Performs fire-fighting duties in the landing zone.

Ship-to-Shore Movement

Embarkation

If the helicopterborne unit is embarked aboard several helicopter transport ships, the HST may also be spread loaded.

Landing

The HST is formed into heli-teams for the ship-to-shore movement. Heli-teams and their equipment normally land in scheduled waves. The position of HST serials in the scheduled waves is determined by the landing plan and they normally land in the following sequence:

- Advance party.
- Helicopter control element.
- HST headquarters (1st echelon).
- Landing zone platoon (1st echelon).
- HST headquarters (2d echelon).
- Landing zone platoon (2d echelon).
- HST equipment.

Operations Ashore

HST operations ashore parallel those of the shore party team. Communications are established as soon as possible between the HST in the landing zone, Navy control agency, supporting TACLOG, helicopterborne unit command section, subsequent helicopter units arriving in the landing zone, adjacent landing zones, and, when a CSS buildup is planned, the LFSP commander. Emergency supplies and troop serials required out of sequence are requested by the helicopterborne unit through the HST commander. The complications of a helicopter assault does not allow the latitude of selection inherent in waterborne assault procedures, and changes to the scheduled movement of units ashore are kept to an absolute minimum. Typically, one HST supports a BLT in a landing zone.

Organization and Function of the Helicopter Landing Zone

The HLZ is organized to effectively accomplish assigned helicopter support tasks. The organization of the landing zone is generally the same as the development of the BSA. However, the helicopter control section replaces the naval beach party within the HLZ. The equipment available for use is limited to that transported into the area by helicopter. Figure 5-3, on page 5-8, illustrates a layout of an HLZ.

Control and Maintenance Facilities

The advance party establishes the landing zone's helicopter control facilities. After the HST is established, the HST's helicopter control section assumes control functions. Personnel provide emergency refueling. If major repairs are required, maintenance personnel and equipment are flown into the landing zone from the helicopter transport ship.

Movement of Supplies

Within the landing zone, troops, equipment, and supplies must be kept clear of the landing area. The movement of supplies is addressed in detail during the planning process. Available transportation is limited; therefore, helicopters place cargo as close to the terminal point as possible. Landing zones must have clear approaches. Dump sites must be adjacent to the landing zone. Adequate equipment and personnel must be available to move incoming supplies rapidly to the dumpsite. Prepackaged supplies are kept within the weight limitations of the HLZ's cargo handling equipment.

Port Operations

A port is any place accessible to ships by seacoast, navigable river or inland waterway that allows the discharge or receipt of cargo. A port operation is the safe, expeditious loading and unloading of equipment, supplies, cargo, and personnel. Port operations involve receiving, processing, and staging of passengers; receiving, moving, storing, and

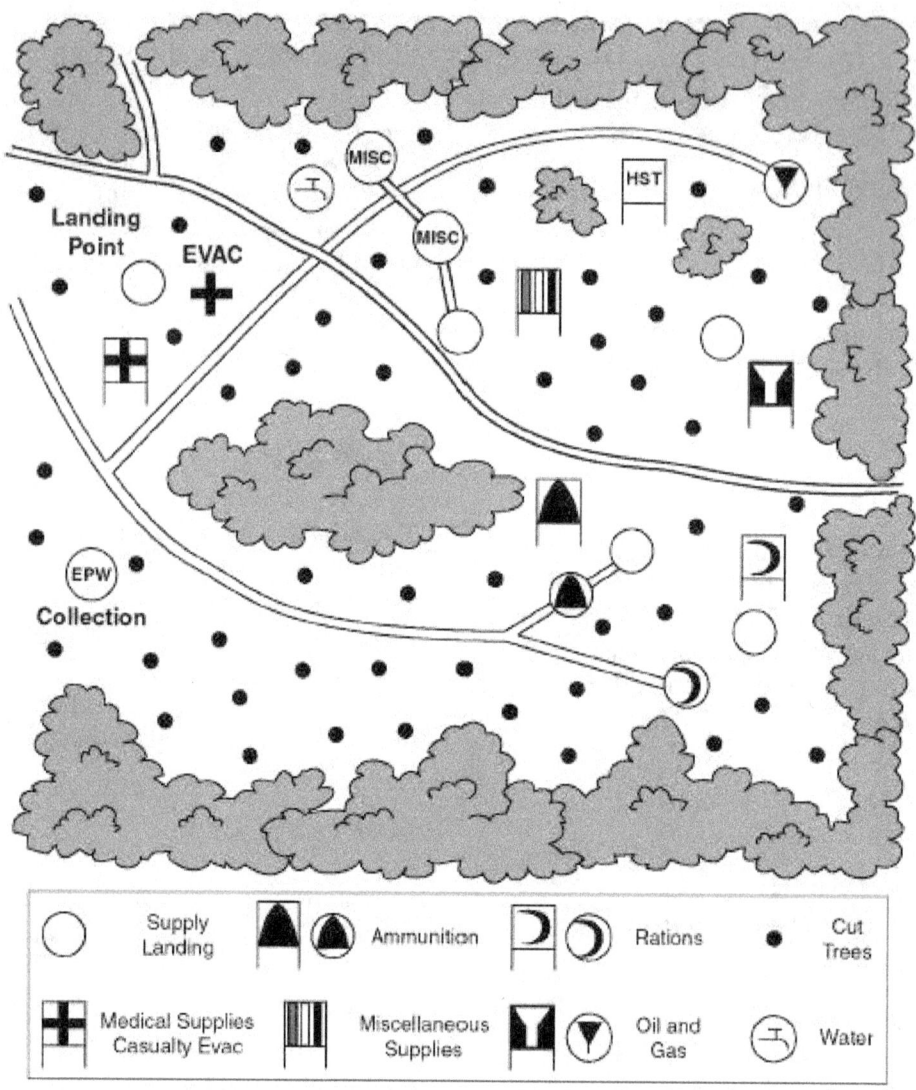

Figure 5-3. Sample Helicopter Landing Zone.

marshalling of cargo; loading and unloading of ships; and lashing, bracing, and shoring of cargo on board ships. Port operations are conducted in an environment that allows emphasis to be placed on safety of the operation rather than the defense of the port and/or safety of personnel and ships.

The unit tasked with the landing support mission in a port operation is the POG. A POG consists of a shore party group and a beach party group just like the LFSP. The port authority's rules and regulations and standing operating procedures guide the POG in its operations. Close coordination among the port operations control group, port authority, and the deploying/redeploying unit is necessary to ensure a smooth throughput of cargo.

Organization

The POG is task-organized around a nucleus from the beach and terminal operations company, TSB. The company provides landing support specialists (MOS 0481) to assist units preparing for deployment/ redeployment. Unit needs and the cargoes moving through the port determine the POG's task organization. Personnel from the unit moving through the port usually augment the POG. If required, additional units, civilian agencies, contracted support (longshoremen and stevedores), and/or host nation support also can augment the POG.

The landing support units that should be in operation during port operations are, at a minimum, the—

- Port command and control center.
- Medical section.
- Preventive medicine section.
- Military police section.
- MHE section.
- Maintenance contact teams.
- Communications teams.
- Bracing and shoring team.
- Staging area coordination teams.

Tasks and Responsibilities

Port Operations Group

The POG's tasks and responsibilities include—

- Providing technical advice to deploying/ redeploying units.
- Providing MHE from the pier staging area to the ship/port crane lifting area or from the ship/port crane drop area to the pier staging area.
- Providing communications for the port operations control group.
- Supervising loading/unloading of gear, agricultural wash-down of tactical equipment in coordination with unit personnel, customs/agricultural officials, and preventive medicine technicians.
- Assisting the loading/unloading unit with the staging of equipment, supplies, and cargo to expedite the loading/staging plan if required.
- Ensuring proper procedures are followed in accordance with JP 3-02.2.

Deploying/Redeploying Unit

The deploying/redeploying unit's tasks and responsibilities include—

- Providing personnel to assist the POG as needed for guard, lashing, bracing, and/or shoring teams.

- Providing embarkation/load plans.
- Providing material for bracing and shoring.
- Coordinating with the POG on embarkation/ debarkation requirements.
- Ensuring equipment meets transportation specifications per JP 3-02.2.

Planning Considerations

Planning is the key to a successful port operation. Planning considerations include—

- Estimating quantities and types of bracing and shoring material needed.
- Training, special equipment, and if additional time is required to load the landing craft.
- Ensuring adequate lighterage required to load ships away from the pier.
- Loading of ships from pier side with the ramp down or with ramp up.

Special considerations for the use of MSC or MSC-chartered ships include the following:

- Coordination requirements with MTMC and MSC.
- The use of civilian longshoremen and stevedores.
- Special needs/restrictions when using MHE aboard MSC ships.
- Dunnage requirements for the ship's ramp.
- Medical support required at the port.
- Vehicle fuel restrictions/requirements.
- Special lifting devices and equipment (i.e., slings, spreader bars).
- Special handling and port regulations for loading ammunition aboard ships.
- ISO container operations.
- Military and commercial transportation requirements at the port.
- Billeting and messing requirements for the POG and for those awaiting movement.
- Head and refuse services.
- Wash-down facilities for agricultural and customs inspections.
- Maintenance contact teams.
- Traffic control in and around the port.

- Access to commercial communications.
- Rail operations at the port.
- Loading, unloading, staging, spills, transportation, and certification of hazardous material.
- Personnel requirements.

Coordination Requirements

Coordinating instructions for a specific operation should be obtained from the port authority/unit embarkation officer and ship's representative (if available). Information is compiled and issued to all arriving/departing units and activities and should contain, at a minimum, the following:

- Ships' docking and scheduled departure times.
- Staging plan.
- Port's hours of operation.
- Civilian longshoremen/stevedores hours.
- MHE support available.
- Lighting requirements.
- Billeting and messing available.
- Communications available.
- Augmentation (drivers, lashing gangs).
- Transportation coordination.
- Medical corpsmen.
- Maintenance contact teams required (this includes wreckers and refueler support).
- MPs. The POG should coordinate with the agencies and organizations listed in table 5-1.

Execution

After the initial planning phase of a port operation has been conducted and guidance has been given concerning the operation, the POG moves to the port 24 hours prior to the deploying unit's or ship's arrival. During this 24-hour period, the POG ensures all POG teams are functional; staging areas are prepared for equipment, vehicles, and cargo; MHE is operational; lines of communications are functioning; and personnel are reminded of local safety procedures and crane and vehicles hand signals.

Table 5-1. POG Points of Contact.

Agency	Services Provided
Navy Port Control	Ship's docking and departure times. Ship's berth. Instream loading and unloading.
Ship's Combat Cargo Officer	Sequence of loading and unloading. Cargo handling equipment (MHE, special slings, etc.). Ship's loading characteristics.
Group Embarkation	Overall plan for loading and unloading. Special lift requirements.
Team Embarkation/MAGTF Embarkation Officer	Copy of load plans and sequence of load.
Port Authority	Security. Use of port cranes. Use of port facilities. Staging areas. Traffic patterns.
Movement Control Center	Update on movement/changes in schedules. Contact teams. Required reports.
Navy Cargo Handling and Port Group	Responsibilities and coordination. Sequence for loading/unloading. Logistic requirements.
Military Traffic Management Command	Responsibilities and coordination. Loading/unloading summary. Special requirements.

Rail Movement Operations

The mission of a rail movement operation is to move personnel and equipment over the existing rail system to their destination. This destination is usually the site where further movement can be accomplished (i.e., pier or airfield) or where owning units can deploy to their areas of responsibility. A rail movement operation involves loading, blocking, bracing, and tie-down of equipment aboard flatcars and other special types of rail cars. Moving units by rail requires detailed planning and preparation by the unit being transported. Rail movement operations are divided into a planning and preparation phase and an execution phase. Coordination is necessary among the moving unit, the traffic management office, the rail facility, the movement control center, and the rail operations team.

Organization

The rail operations team is task-organized around a nucleus from the beach and terminal operations company, TSB. The needs of the units moving through the rail yard determine the rail operations team's task organization. Liaison/interpreter elements may be required if conducting rail movement operations in a foreign country. The organizational structure should provide, at a minimum, the following sections:

- Command/administration.
- Operations.
- Materials handling equipment.
- Motor transport.
- Traffic control.
- Communications.
- Loading/blocking and bracing teams.
- Maintenance, supply, and medical.
- Rail inspection.
- Security.
- Host nation liaison/interpreter if required.

Tasks and Responsibilities

Rail Operations Team

The rail operations team's mission is to plan for, coordinate, and supervise the loading and unloading of rail cars in support of deploying/redeploying units. The rail operations team establishes itself at the railhead to coordinate and ensure the throughput of the deploying unit. In conjunction with the deploying unit, the rail operations team plans and executes the staging, movement to the railhead, and the departure of moving units. The rail operations team's duties include—

- Providing technical rail loading/unloading expertise.
- Providing technical data on rail cars.
- Determining blocking and bracing material requirements.
- Computing rail car requirements based on unit movement data.
- Conducting the receiving inspection on the serviceability of rail cars.

- Providing an inspection team to ensure the quality of blocking and bracing.
- Providing a GBL.
- Checking and obtaining route clearances for overweight or outsized items.
- Training of personnel.

Deploying Unit

The deploying unit is responsible for—

- Loading/unloading the rail cars.
- Meeting the unit movement date.
- Preparing for movement.
- Planning, supervising, and executing movement from unit staging area to call forward area to rail siding.
- Purchasing and providing material to be used in blocking and bracing equipment.
- Identifying unique restrictions or requirements of selected equipment.
- Processing of personnel.

Planning Considerations

The planning and preparation phase can be further subdivided into preplanning, detailed planning, and preparation of equipment. The Association of American Railroads loading rules are used as a guide during planning. The unit movement officer should use the planning phase of rail movement operations to validate and confirm rail equipment requirements, establish/verify timetables and schedules, and simplify the load as much as possible.

Preplanning

During the planning and preparation phase, the unit movement officer should—

- List all equipment to be transported (including loaded dimensions and loaded weight).
- Establish liaison with rail authorities/traffic management office representatives and rail operations team to identify rail equipment available.
- Determine capabilities of rail sidings to be used.

Detailed Planning

During the detailed planning phase, the specific rules listed in the Association of American Railroads' loading rules and the guidance provided by the traffic management office and the rail operations team must be followed. The unit movement officer and the rail operations team must work closely during planning for the unit's movement by rail. The following concepts are used for guidance:

- Avoid mixing tracked and wheeled vehicles on the same car (higher tariffs are charged for this configuration).
- Use 100,000 pounds as a load limit on all cars.
- Limit width to 100 inches, if possible, because of clearances.
- Know height restrictions and coordinate alternative transportation for equipment that is too tall.
- Know the different types and capacities of rail cars.
- Sequence the vehicles to be loaded.
- Template the load. Establish a call forward plan.
- Plan for unloading: Is there a spur at the final destination? ramps? MHE?

Preparation of Equipment

During this phase, the deploying unit must prepare all equipment and vehicles for loading in accordance with established guidance. The deploying unit ensures that all personnel involved in the movement know the sequence of movement from the unit staging area to the call forward area and then to the rail siding.

Coordination Requirements

Without coordination, equipment can easily be lost or sent on the wrong trains. Coordination helps prevent confusion that can easily lead to injuries or damage to equipment.

Execution

The execution phase is the culmination of all planning and preparation. The actual loading and bracing of the equipment on the rail cars takes time, and safety should be a prime concern.

Motor Transport Operations

Marine Forces may be employed in areas of extremes in weather and terrain. These areas encompass more than half the earth's land surface and are made up of arctic-like areas, mountains, deserts, jungles, and flooded areas. Additionally, improved technology and dramatic increase of mobile forces worldwide require the Marine Corps to be prepared to conduct mobile operations consistent with current maneuver concepts. In support of mobile maneuver forces in areas of extreme weather or terrain, normal motor transport procedures will require modification to be effective. For convoy operations, refer to MCRP 4-11.3F, *Convoy Operations Handbook*.

Jungle Operations

Jungle terrain includes areas of tropical rain forest and secondary growth that vary in locale from mountains to low-lying swampy plains. It lacks fully developed LOCs. Jungle terrain and climate limit foot and vehicular movement, observation, fields of fire, communications, and control. There are few roads and trails in jungle areas and their use is limited to light trucks or tracked vehicles. Roads usually have to be constructed, but the dense vegetation, unstable soils, poor drainage, and general lack of building materials make road building difficult. Jungle roads and trails are overgrown rapidly unless they are in constant use. Extensive reconnaissance and/or clearing may be necessary to locate and put roads to use.

Planning for Jungle Operations

Light vehicles provide greater utility when operating on jungle trails and roads. Additionally, the load-bearing capacity of the soil in most jungle areas, especially during the rainy season, is quite low. Extensive engineer effort may be anticipated to maintain any roads that carry heavy vehicles. Distances may be short, but operating speeds will be low; therefore, movement planning must compensate for this limiting factor. During and after rains, roads will quickly become impassable if subject to heavy traffic flow. Movements in hostile areas require effective security measures to guard against ambush. Seasonal weather conditions will affect all aspects of motor transport operations. Become familiar with the area weather and prepare for the worst.

Driving Techniques

Normal driving techniques are employed in jungle operations. However, operators must be oriented to the jungle environment; they must be on guard to avoid areas their vehicles are incapable of passing and the possibility of flooding in low areas and along watercourses during heavy rains.

On unimproved roads, except in high mine threat areas, vehicles should not follow in the preceding vehicle's tire tracks. Doing so leads to the development of ruts, drainage problems, and reduced trafficability.

The reduced visibility that is characteristic of jungle roads requires operators to be alert and prepare for defensive action against enemy threats and road hazards.

Operators watch for overheating of vehicles as a result of prolonged low speed operation or radiator blockage from mud or vegetation.

Desert Operations

Deserts are semiarid and arid regions containing a wide variety of soils in varying relief. Desert characteristics include extreme temperatures, dust storms, lack of water and vegetation, bright sunshine and moonlight, mirages, and lack of roads. The dynamic nature of desert operations, and the large areas in which they may be conducted, necessitate some modification of landing force organization and equipment to provide for increased mobility. Desert operations can be most efficiently conducted when the landing force is 100 percent mobile. Planners should be concerned with integrating available motor transport, amphibious assault vehicles, light armor vehicles, tanks, self-propelled weapons, and aircraft into a combination that will best support the landing force.

Planning for Desert Operations

Operations in the desert involve long distances and are conducted over terrain that channels motor transport movements.

There are few developed roads and the similarity of terrain features makes cross-country navigation difficult. Therefore, motor transport personnel must have maps and be proficient in land navigation techniques. Marines should receive training with the precision lightweight global positioning system (GPS) receiver (PLGR) and use its capabilities to the fullest while navigating in the desert.

Vehicles should be well dispersed during movements and at halts as a defense against air and artillery attacks.

Camouflage materials should be carried on vehicles since there will normally be little natural concealment.

The desert climate will reduce the ability of personnel to perform physically. In some cases, especially over the long term, it will be counter-productive to attempt heavy labor except during the most favorable times of the day or night. Maintenance of vehicles exposed to the sun in hot desert areas must be limited to essential tasks. Shelter may be required to provide shade. Maintenance activities may have to be scheduled during hours of darkness.

Vehicles with poor cross-country mobility should not be employed in the desert. Consideration should be made to travel at night as to avoid visual detection from low flying aircraft and ground forces. All Marines should use every available tool and receive training in night driving techniques (i.e., blackout lights, night vision goggles [NVGs], and PLGRs).

Driving Techniques

Driving in intense heat over long distances and for extended periods of time will be monotonous and tiring. High-speed operation on desert roads will require operators to remain alert in spite of the monotony. Each vehicle in a convoy will raise a cloud of dust, which will obscure the vision of the following operator, therefore, vehicle spacing should be increased to the maximum extent possible consistent with convoy security. The following techniques should be used:

- Wear goggles while driving open hatched vehicles regardless of visibility. Clear-lens goggles should be worn at night unless NVGs are used. Bandannas

5-14 ————————————————————————————————— MCWP 4-11.3

or surgical masks should be worn to avoid breathing heavy dust.

- Maintain a dust distance of twice the normal interval, or as specified in the unit SOP to allow time for the dust to dissipate. When driving on extremely dusty roads or trails and, if traffic conditions permit, a staggered column formation can be used with vehicles alternately driving on the left and right side of the road.

- Turn on lights to increase visibility. Overtaking and passing slower vehicles should be accomplished with great care when dust obscures the roadway and possible oncoming vehicles under dusty conditions.

- Remain alert and adjust speed to keep engine revolutions per minute within the safe operating range. Fuel consumption will increase dramatically. Although the desert may appear to be flat, gradually rising terrain will often make it impossible to operate at highest gear range and at the proper engine revolutions per minute. A strong headwind will compound this problem as will a covering of loose sand on the roadway.

- Drive on sand at night or early morning when the sand is damp and traction is better. However, this is not always the case especially with the newer type military tires with closer tread design. Damp sand packs between the tread in the grooves of these tires resulting in virtually no surface traction. While driving in loose sand, the vehicle tends to get mired down. The best thing to do is use low transfer and low gears to keep vehicle engine and transmission from over heating. It is best to reduce vehicle tire pressure to the recommended tire pressure listed in the vehicles technical manuals for that specific vehicle. Vehicle speed should be reduced when tire pressure is reduced. Lower tire pressure at higher speeds increase tire sidewall heat and will increase the possibility of tire failure. The lower tire pressure does not affect vehicles equipped with radial tires or central tire inflation system if the maximum speed listed in the operator's manual is not exceeded.

- Vehicle loads must be evenly distributed. All-wheel drive should be used where possible to prevent the vehicle becoming mired down.

Mountain Operations

In mountain areas, conditions of ground and climate require modification in landing force and motor transport organization, training, equipment, and tactics. Mountains cause compartmentalization of military operations and present great difficulties to movement and maneuver. The weather is characterized by rapid changes in temperature accompanied by high wind fog, mist, rain or snow. Road nets are limited and the construction of new roads and trails is difficult and time-consuming. Even when road nets are available, the enemy may hinder movement by destroying bridges, chartered sections of the road along steep slopes or blocking defiles with slides of snow, rocks or timber. Vehicles are used as far forward as possible, then supplies are moved forward on animals or porters in steeper, more inaccessible country. Within density-altitude limitations, helicopters may be used for moving equipment and supplies. Airdrop of supplies and equipment may be necessary when flying conditions permit.

Planning for Mountain Operations

Specific knowledge of road characteristics is especially important in mountains. Grades, bridge capacities, tunnels, and the radius of turns may limit the types of vehicles that can be employed, as well as the loads they can carry.

Seasonal weather patterns of the AO should be reviewed. At high altitudes, freezing rain and snow can be expected over a major portion of the year. The motor transport officer should evaluate potential weather conditions and prepare for the worst.

Unless a well-developed road net is available, heavy vehicles and certain truck-trailer combinations may be useless in the mountains.

Recovery of disabled vehicles will be difficult and may completely halt the flow of traffic. Before operation checks, maintenance and inspection of vehicles prior to dispatch must be closely monitored.

Driving Techniques

Marine Corps vehicles are well-suited to operating in mountainous regions due to their high power-to-weight ratios, low-gear ratios, and relatively short wheelbase. Operators should have no difficulty in operating vehicles on the steep grades, sharp curves, and narrow roadways if vehicles are checked for mechanical fitness prior to being dispatched, loaded within prescribed limits, and driven skillfully with full concern for road and weather conditions.

When approaching a steep upgrade, especially when loaded, the operator should make a judgment as to whether the high-gear or low-gear range will be required. Normally, the lowest range will be used and the transfer case should be shifted to low range before the vehicle speed drops below that prescribed by the respective technical manual. This will increase chances of topping the hill at best possible speed and with the engine operating at maximum torque speed. This early shift of the transfer case into lower gear range will often avoid having to shift into first gear at low speeds when driving manual shift vehicles. On vehicles with an automatic transmission, it will prevent overheating of the transmission fluid.

When approaching a downgrade, the operator should make a judgment as to what gear should be used to obtain the best retarding effect from the engine. Brakes should be tested, brake air pressure monitored, and the vehicle speed reduced to a rate consistent with road and weather conditions. In the event that brakes fail and the engine retarding capability is exceeded, emergency stop procedures should be executed immediately including, if necessary, ditching the vehicle on the uphill side of the road. Attempting to ride it out on a runaway vehicle adds to the chances of serious injury and endangers other vehicles and personnel.

Cold Weather Operations

Operations in arctic and sub-arctic regions of the world require a landing force and its transportation elements to use special equipment and special techniques to operate successfully. Deep snow and extreme cold are also found in the north temperate zone and at high altitudes in all zones. The areas in which these conditions exist range from forested to relatively barren regions and vary extensively in population. Offensive and defensive operations in these areas are conducted as in other climates. However, operations require greater CSS, more time to accomplish, more attention to detail, and more effective leadership. The considerations of special

techniques and equipment must be included in the conduct of such operations.

Planning for Cold Weather Operations

In-depth planning for motor transport operations is necessary and must provide for reduced capability of vehicles and motor transport units.

Special training for operators in cold weather driving and vehicle maintenance is essential when providing motor transport services to units engaged in cold weather warfare.

Routes with easily identifiable checkpoints should be used. Checkpoints require pronounced vertical characteristics, since drifting snow covers contours and terrain features rapidly. An assistant operator should be assigned to each vehicle. Driving in heavy snow and deep cold is fatiguing and demands increased driver concentration that makes periodic relief necessary.

All vehicles must have proper tires, chains, tow devices, and snow shovels.

Items likely to be needed first should be loaded last.

Low temperatures require increased maintenance personnel, facilities, and special equipment. Low-temperature lubricants and fuels must be provided. Shelter from the wind and intense cold is required for performance of any but the simplest maintenance tasks.

Motor vehicle operators and crew must be equipped with and required to carry cold weather clothing and equipment in their vehicles for survival in case of accident or breakdown. They must be trained to survive in the cold.

Units engaged in cold weather warfare require additional vehicles, and vehicles are less efficient for the following reasons:

- Organic vehicles of the units have reduced capability thereby placing increased demands on support units.
- Vehicles require extra time and special attention for starting at low temperatures.

- The number of troops that can be transported in vehicles will be reduced due to bulk of clothing and additional gear carried. The quantity of individual and organizational equipment required to survive in cold climates makes it necessary for the unit to use a greater number of vehicles to transport the unit load.

- Operating speeds are reduced to accommodate hazardous driving conditions.

- Fuel consumption is increased by 25 to 50 percent due to operation in lower gears, increased idle time to warm running gear, and frequent starting and stopping due to hazardous road conditions.

- Frequency of accidents and enroute delays are increased by hazardous road conditions.

- Bad weather conditions and fatigue of cargo handlers will increase loading and unloading times.

The capability of motor transport units to provide increased support will be influenced by the existence of the same degrading factors enumerated above for organic transport operations. In addition it must be expected that the availability of vehicles for service will deteriorate as a function of the duration and the intensity of cold weather.

The level of maintenance of the road net in heavy snow areas will have strong influence on the support capabilities of the motor transport units, especially in performing resupply missions. Snow clearing must be planned for and equipment must be available to support motor transport units.

Tactical employment of infantry units will require them to operate off the established road net. Infantry units require support of marginal terrain vehicles to retain their mobility despite the heavy additional loads imposed by clothing, shelter, fuel to heat shelters, and increased quantity of rations. The vehicles, in turn, increase supply and maintenance needs of the units.

Maintained Road Net

Convoy operations may be carried out normally, except for reduced speeds and increased gaps between vehicles. Convoy speed is adjusted dependent upon the road surface conditions along various sections of the route or changes in weather conditions. Vehicle operators are trained to keep the other vehicles in the group in sight and assist if a vehicle becomes disabled.

Unmaintained Road Net

On roads not fully maintained by snow removal operations, vehicles in the 1 1/4 -ton class can operate at reduced speeds in snow depths up to 6 inches. Vehicles in the 5-ton payload class can operate at reduced speeds in snow up to 12 inches deep and under emergency conditions with full payload in snow depths of 20 inches with fully trained and experienced operators. Use of non-powered trailers or other towed loads should be avoided in heavy snow conditions.

Ice

Frozen lakes and rivers are excellent supply routes. Ice routes must be selected and tested for ice thickness and structural integrity. Even amphibious vehicles may not be able to extricate themselves from an ice hole (see table 5-2).

Oversnow Vehicles

Operation of oversnow logistics support vehicles require special procedures to ensure maximum use of every vehicle.

The following principles apply:

- Use prepared and marked trails whenever possible.

- Dispatch vehicles in small groups, never singly.

- Exercise positive control measures to monitor the location of every vehicle operating off trails.

- Train operators to be proficient in land navigation when operating cross-country.

- Top off fuel tanks when dispatching a vehicle to ensure sufficient range for the return trip.

- Minimize operations on cleared roads.

- Tow a sled rather then overload the vehicle in deep snow.

- Observe care when transporting troops. Closed oversnow vehicles are prone to entrapment of carbon monoxide.

Table 5-2. Ice Load-Bearing Capacities.

Load Type	Gross Weight (tons)	Minimum Ice Thickness (cm/in)	Minimum Distance Between Loads (meters/yards)
Marine on Skis or Snowshoes	0.1	3/1.2	5/5.5
Marine on Foot	0.1	5/2	5/5.5
Infantry (column of 2)		7.6/3	7.3/8
Infantry (column of 4)		10/4	10/11
Wheeled Vehicle Loads up to:	3.5	23/9	15/16.5
	6	30/12	20/22
	10	40/16	25.6/28
	15	61/24	30/33
Tracked Vehicles Loads up to:	3.5	20/8	15/16.5
	10	30/12	20/22
	12.5	40/16	25.6/28
	25	61/24	40/44
	45	81/32	50/55
	60	81/32	60/66

Mobile Operations

Maneuver is the movement of forces to secure or retain positional advantage over an enemy. The GCE commander may require motor transport assets in addition to amphibious vehicles, armored vehicles, and helicopters to achieve the ground battlefield mobility required by the tactical situation.

Employment

The continuous requirements for timely concentration of units and material will often demand short notice movement of forces and major shifts in movement direction. Motor transport units should be attached to maneuver units during mobile operations to provide unity of command that will increase responsiveness and flexibility.

Operations

During these types of operations, trucks will be used to move infantry companies and their equipment rapidly to dismount points to continue the attack on foot. As objectives are seized, trucks will be called forward under the leadership of motor transport leaders and infantry units will remount the trucks and continue the attack in an effort to maintain the momentum of the attack. Traditional convoy techniques may not be employed under these conditions. Motor transport unit leaders will be required to advise and assist infantry unit leaders in developing plans including movement formations, movement techniques, and primary and alternate routes to objectives and dismount points. Motor transport leaders will also be required to advise infantry leaders on the maintenance of vehicles.

Mechanized Operations

Mechanized operations are conducted by infantry units mounted in amphibious assault vehicles (AAVs), supported by armor, along with a full combined arms team of combat support and CSS elements. Mechanized operations will be characterized by rapid, long-distance movements and requirements for great amounts of supplies. In order to sustain mechanized operations and maintain the momentum of the attack, logistics trains will be formed for the maneuver units. Unlike tank and artillery units, infantry units do not have organic medium trucks that will be required in the logistic trains.

Employment

Mechanized operations will be fast moving and will often move well forward of friendly units or in unanticipated directions to take advantage of a tactical situation. Motor transport units should be attached to infantry battalions to meet the lift requirements of the logistic trains.

Operations

Motor transport unit leaders should retain tactical command of their trucks while under the command of the commander of the logistic train. In this role, the motor transport leader also advises and assists the logistic commander in the planning of convoy procedures and movement routes for the logistic train and routes for resupply of forward combat units.

APPENDIX A. BEACH AND LANDING SITE MARKERS

- **Unloading Point Markers** -

**Medical Supplies
Casualty Evacuation**

Day

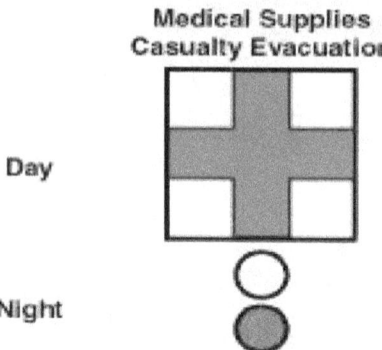

Night

**Lights and Markers for
- - - - - - - - - - - Use and Control of Amphibious Vehicles** - - - - - - - - - - -

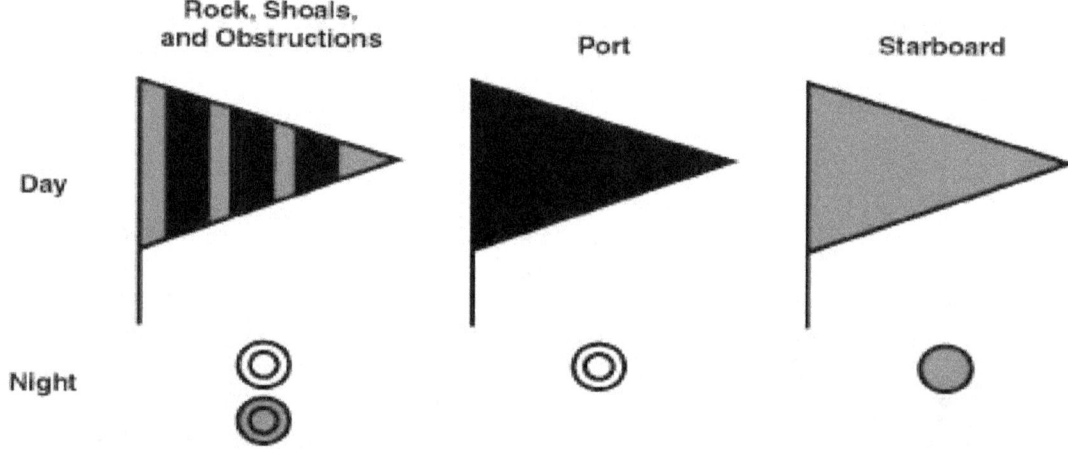

Rock, Shoals,
and Obstructions   Port   Starboard

Day

Night

- **Numeral Flags** -

One	Two	Three	Four

Five	Six	Seven	Eight

Nine	Ten

- **Miscellaneous Flags** -

W	S	Y
Assistant Boat Group Commander	**Salvage Boat**	**LVT Pool Control Officer**

---------------------------- Miscellaneous Flags ----------------------------

N

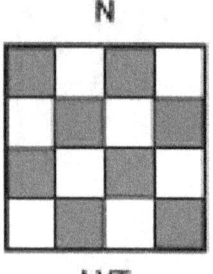

LVT
Emergency

T

Transfer Line
Control Officer

B

Bowser Boat

M

Medical Boat

---------------------------- Miscellaneous Beach Flags ----------------------------

Dud Flag

Mine Cleared
Area

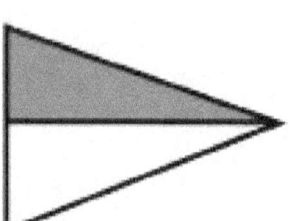

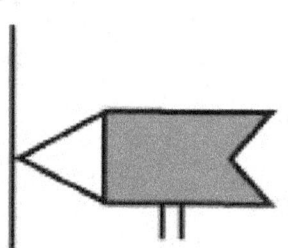

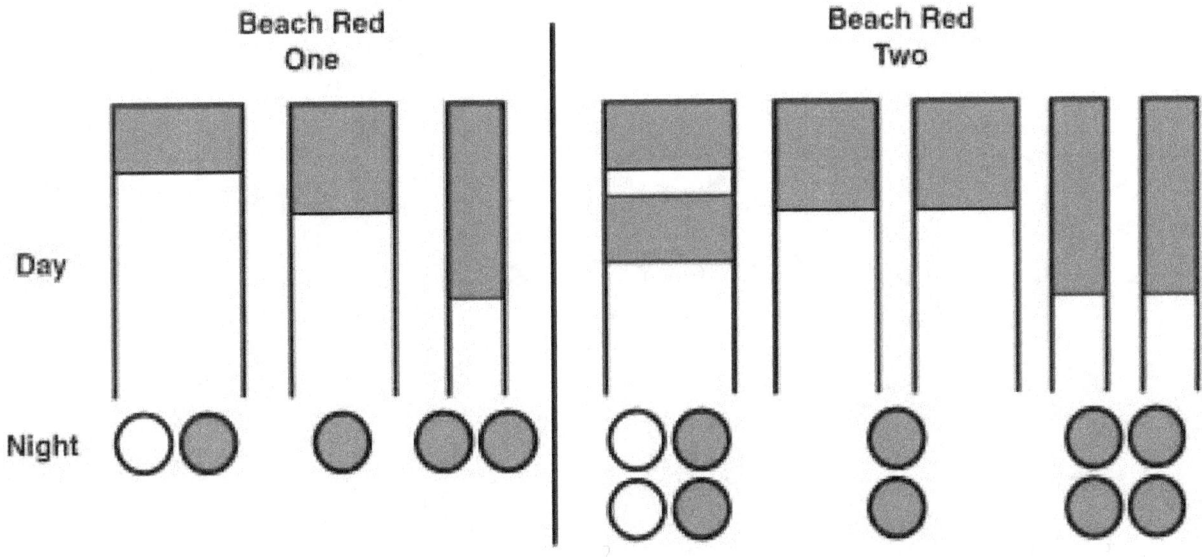

Beach Markers (from Seaward)

APPENDIX B. DEPARTURE AIRFIELD CONTROL GROUP CHECKLIST

The following is a checklist designed to assist the DACG in the performance of its mission. The following tasks should not be overlooked during planning. The tasks listed are not all inclusive, but are intended as a guide.

- Brief personnel engaged in DACG operations.

- Establish required communications.

- Secure parking and flow plan from TALCE.

- Brief unit commanders on vehicle flow plan.

- Ensure that sufficient load team personnel with pusher vehicles are available.

- Coordinate with the TALCE to ensure that personnel and cargo are guided to the proper aircraft.

- Inform liaison officers to changes to movement plan.

- Maintain status of arrival, departure, and loading.

- Obtain airfield diagrams for guides.

- Ensure that communications are operational between all elements of the DACG.

- Ensure that support equipment, wreckers, POLs, food service, lighting, first aid, weighing devices, and maintenance contact teams are available.

- Coordinate with the MAGTF operations officer.

- Coordinate with the deploying units' movement officer.

- Coordinate with the call forward officer.

- Issue special instructions to alerted aircraft loads.

- Receive instructions from the MAGTF/deploying unit operations officer.

- Inspect all loads upon receipt from the alert holding area.

- Assist in preparing, inspecting, and making corrections as necessary to passenger and cargo manifests.

- Provide guides to escort planeloads through the loading ramp area to designated plane sites or release points.

- Inform MAGTF/deploying unit operations officer of problems affecting movement schedules.

- Coordinate with the TALCE to ensure aircraft are parked and assigned numbers in accordance with the movement plan.

- Coordinate MHE with the TALCE.

- Unload personnel/equipment from aborted aircraft and guide to replacement aircraft or holding area.

- Ensure all personnel involved in the movement operation are briefed on safety.

- Ensure all incidents/accidents are investigated and reported.

- Ensure that personal and related services are provided by the base/installation for deploying unit(s).

- Ensure logistics requirements are met.

- Provide deploying unit(s) with points of contact for logistics support.

- Secure and supervise facilities for the DACG and deploying unit(s).

- Compile pertinent deployment and movement data.

- Coordinate reports required by higher headquarters/ movement control centers with the TALCE.

APPENDIX C. ARRIVAL AIRFIELD CONTROL GROUP CHECKLIST

The following is a checklist designed to assist the AACG in the performance of its mission. The following tasks should not be overlooked during planning. The tasks listed are not all inclusive, but are intended as a guide.

- Brief all personnel engaged in AACG operations.

- Establish required communications.

- Secure parking and flow plan from TALCE.

- Ensure that sufficient offload team personnel with pusher vehicles are available.

- Coordinate with the TALCE to ensure that personnel and cargo are cleared from arriving aircraft and guided to release point or holding area.

- Maintain status of the arrival and departure of the deploying unit's personnel and equipment at the arrival airfield.

- Ensure that dunnage/shoring materials are retained by the deploying unit.

- Coordinate with the MAGTF operations officer.

- Coordinate with the deploying units' movement officer.

- Inform MAGTF/deploying unit operations officer of problems affecting movement schedules.

- Coordinate MHE with the DACG and the TALCE.

- Ensure all personnel involved in the movement operation are briefed on safety.

- Ensure all incidents/accidents are investigated and reported.

- Ensure that personal and related services are provided by the base/installation for deploying unit(s).

- Ensure logistics requirements are met.

- Provide deploying unit(s) with points of contact for logistics support.

- Compile pertinent deployment and movement data.

- Coordinate reports required by higher headquarters/ movement control centers with the TALCE.

APPENDIX D. DEPLOYING UNIT AND D/AACG PLANNING AND PREPARATION PHASE REQUIREMENTS

The following is a checklist designed to assist the DACG in the performance of its mission. The following tasks should not be overlooked during planning. The tasks listed are not all inclusive, but are intended as a guide.

Deploying Unit Tasks

- Identify the number of personnel to be moved.

- Identify the type and quantity of cargo and equipment to be moved.

- Establish priorities for arrival.

- Establish required liaison.

- Identify the cargoes or equipment that require special handling based on shipping configuration or fragile/hazardous characteristics.

- Request technical assistance.

- Prepare equipment and train personnel.

- Request staff assistance in administrative support, unit movement training, air movement planning, logistics, and maintenance support and standard safety practices in and around aircraft.

- Assign unit movement or embarkation officer.

- Develop traffic plan for movement to the departure airfield.

- Establish trained load teams to assist the D/AACG.

- Identify foreign border clearance requirements if applicable.

- Enter force deployment requirements into the Joint Planning and Execution System (JOPES) to accurately reflect lift requirements and deployment priorities.

- Review inspection procedures and documentation requirements for hazardous cargo.

- Coordinate procedures for transporting individual weapons, ammunition, and equipment.

- Determine shoring requirements, ensure its availability prior to loading, and establish destination disposition procedures.

- Construct 463L pallets in accordance with FMFM 4-6, *Movements of Units in Air Force Aircraft*.

- Prepare vehicles and equipment in accordance with FMFM 4-6.

DACG Tasks

- Determine the number of personnel to be moved.

- Determine the type and quantity of cargo and equipment to be moved.

- Determine the timeframe for loading.

- Confirm the location of airfield(s) and marshaling area(s) with the installation or base commander and the deploying unit.

- Determine available departure airfield logistics/ administrative facilities.

- Develop DACG organization structure and staffing.

- Determine user support requirements (MHE, security, lighting, fuels, etc.)

- Establish liaison with the deploying unit and other support activities.

- Coordinate with the TALCE to establish DACG training requirements.

- Coordinate foreign border clearance requirements and procedures if necessary.

- Obtain unit deployment list (UDL) of unit cargo and equipment to be loaded. Identify any problems that will affect loading or require special attention to the TALCE.

- Validate shoring requirements.

- Ensure 463L pallet dunnage availability.

- Determine requirements for vehicle cargo restraint devices based on deployed unit input.

AACG Tasks

- Coordinate with TALCE prior to arrival of aircraft to determine support requirements.

- Ascertain the unloading timeframe.

- Determine location of arrival airfield(s) and holding area(s).

- Determine AACG logistics/administrative facilities available at the arrival airfield.

- Develop AACG organizational structure and staff.

- Establish liaison with deploying unit, TALCE, and other supporting activities.

- Coordinate with the TALCE to establish AACG training requirements.

- Confirm coordination contacts.

- Obtain UDL of unit cargo and equipment to be loaded. Identify any problems that will affect loading or require special attention to the TALCE.

- Finalize AACG organization to include aircraft load teams and training requirements.

APPENDIX E. DEPLOYING UNIT AND D/AACG REQUIREMENTS DURING THE EXECUTION PHASE

Deploying Unit Tasks (At the Departure Airfield)

- Establish liaison with the DACG and other activities.

- Conduct final preparation of vehicles, cargo, and equipment in accordance with FMFM 4-6.

- Ensure required shoring is on-hand.

- Prepare cargo and passenger manifests in accordance with FMFM 4-6.

- Assemble personnel, cargo, and equipment in aircraft loads per established load plans.

- Appoint plane team commanders and brief on responsibilities.

- Pass control of unit aircraft loads to DACG at the alert holding area at the time specified by the DACG.

- Correct discrepancies identified by the DACG and TALCE during Joint Inspection.

- Provide specialized help in loading the aircraft if required.

- Retain one copy of final passenger/cargo manifests.

- At the arrival airfield, the deploying unit will—

  - Provide assistance to the loadmaster.

  - Receive instructions from the unload team chief.

  - Retain or dispose of all shoring and dunnage as determined in planning.

DACG Tasks

- Maintain liaison with the deploying unit.

- Arrange technical assistance required by the deploying unit with the TALCE.

- Maintain liaison with the aerial port section.

- Call aircraft loads forward from the marshaling area and assume control in the alert holding area.

- Inspect aircraft loads and ensure they are complete and correctly prepared and that the required shoring and dunnage was provided by the deploying unit.

- Establish a discrepancy correction area.

- Inspect documentation for accuracy and completeness.

- Ensure passenger accountability and control.

- Provide emergency maintenance and related services, as necessary, to accomplish the loading mission.

- Direct aircraft loads to the call forward area when required.

- Assist in the joint inspection of aircraft loads.

- Ensure the deploying unit corrects discrepancies found during the joint inspection.

- Move equipment forward to the ready line when required.

- Reassemble aircraft loads, with the assistance of the TALCE, and prepare required manifest changes if there are aircraft aborts, changes or ACL discrepancies.

- Maintain statistical data on the movement of personnel and equipment, as well as passenger/cargo manifests and inspection records.

- Ensure the deploying unit adheres to the established timetable.

- Provide loading team personnel and support equipment.

- Provide fueling/defueling capability.

- Provide emergency maintenance for vehicles to be transported.

- Provide and control passenger-holding area if required.

- Transfer control of the aircraft load to the TALCE at the ready line and monitor the loading.

- Obtain aircraft load completion time from the TALCE.

Load Team Chief Tasks (at the ready line)—

- Receive the load at the ready line.

- Direct and supervise load teams and vehicle operators.

- Ensure equipment and supplies are properly restrained in the aircraft.

- Coordinate with the TALCE ready line coordinator for any special assistance or support needed.

- Ensure loadmaster has appropriate number of copies of passenger/cargo manifest.

- Conduct preflight briefing to all embarking personnel.

- Pass load completion time to the TALCE's AOC section.

AACG Tasks

- Establish coordination with the receiving command or installation if the AACG is part of the arriving unit's load element.

- Ensure accountable aircraft restraint devices are returned to the aircraft.

- Establish liaison and maintain coordination with the deploying unit and the TALCE.

- Ensure unload teams are available and briefed on their duties.

- Coordinate with the TALCE and the deploying unit on the recovery and storage of shoring and dunnage.

- Accept each planeload from the TALCE at the established release point.

- Establish facilities as determined during planning.

- Maintain records on personnel and cargo received and cleared.

- Release aircraft load to the deploying unit at the designated location.

APPENDIX F. GLOSSARY

SECTION I. ACRONYMS AND ABBREVIATIONS

A

AAA . . . . arrival and assembly area

AACG . . . . arrival airfield control group

AAFS . . . . amphibious assault fuel system

AALPS . . Automated Aircraft Load Planning System

AAOE . . . . . arrival and assembly operations element

AAOG . . . . arrival and assembly operations group

AAV . . . . amphibious assault vehicle

ABCA   American, British, Canadian, Australian Armies Standardization Program

ACE . . . . aviation combat element

ACO . . . . airfield coordination officer

A/DACG . . . . . arrival/departure airfield control group

ADCON . . . . administrative control

AFOE . . . . assault follow-on echelon

AIS . . . . automated information system

AMC . . . . Air Mobility Command

ANSI . . . . American National Standards Institute

AO . . . . area of operations

AOR . . . . area of responsibility

A/SPOD . . . . air and/or sea ports of debarkation

A/SPOE . . . . air and/or sea ports of embarkation

ATF . . . . amphibious task force

ATLASS . . . . asset tracking for logistics and supply system

B

BLT . . . . battalion landing team

BOG . . . . beach operations group

BSA . . . . beach support area

C

C2 . . . . command and control

CAEMS . . . . computer-aided embarkation management system

CALM . . . . Computer-Aided Load Manifesting

CAPS II . . . . consolidated aerial ports system II

CATF . . . . commander, amphibious task force

CE . . . . command element

CINC . . . . commander in chief

CLF . . . . commander, landing force

CLZ . . . . craft landing zone

cm . . . . centimeter

CNSE . . . . commander, naval support element

CONUS . . . . continental United States

CSS . . . . combat service support

CSSE . . . . combat service support element

D

DACG . . . . departure airfield control group

DCD . . . . data collection device

DLA . . . . Defense Logistics Agency

DOD . . . . Department of Defense

DS . . . . direct support

DTG . . . . date-time group

DTS . . . . Defense Transportation System

E

EPW . . . . enemy prisoner of war

ERP . . . . equipment reception point

evac . . . . evacuation

F

FARP . . . . forward arming and refueling point

FIE . . . . fly-in echelon

FMCC . . . . force movement control center

FMFM . . . . Fleet Marine Force manual

FOSAMS . . . . fleet optical scanning ammunition marking system

FSSG . . . . force service support group

FW . . . . fixed wing

G

G-1/S-1 . . . . manpower or personnel officer

G-3/S-3 . . . . operations staff officer

G-4/S-4 . . . . logistics staff officer

GBL . . . . government bill of lading
GCCS . . . . global command and control system
GCE . . . . ground combat element
GDSS . . . . Global Decision Support System
GS . . . . general support
GTN . . . . Global Transportation Network

H

HQ . . . . headquarters
HHQ . . . . higher headquarters
HLZ . . . . helicopter landing zone
HST . . . . helicopter support team

I

ISO . . . . . . International Standardization Organization
in . . . . inch
ITV . . . . in-transit visibility

J

JFAST . . . . Joint Flow and Analysis System
for Transportation
JFC . . . . joint force commander
JIATF . . . . joint interagency task force
JLOTS . . . . joint logistics over-the-shore
JMC . . . . joint movement center
JOPES . . . . Joint Operation Planning and
Execution System
JP . . . . joint publication
JTF . . . . joint task force

L

LCAC . . . . landing craft air cushion
LFSP . . . . landing force support party
LMCC . . . . logistic movement control center
LOC . . . . lines of communications
LOGSAFE . . . . logistics sustainment analysis and
feasibility estimator
LOGMARS . . . . . . logistics applications of automated
marking and reading symbols
LVS . . . . Logistics Vehicle System
LVT . . . . landing vehicle track
LZSA . . . . landing zone support area

M

MAGTF . . . . Marine air-ground task force
MAGTF II/LOG AIS . . . . Marine air-ground task
force II/logistics automated
information system
MARFOR . . . . Marine Corps forces
MAW . . . . Marine aircraft wing
MCC . . . . movement control center
MCWP . . . . . . Marine Corps warfighting publication
MDL . . . . MAGTF Data Library
MDSS II . . . MAGTF Deployment Support System II
MEF . . . . Marine expeditionary force
MHE . . . . materials handling equipment
MOMAT . . . . mobility matting
MOS . . . . military occupational speciality
MP . . . . military police
MPE/S . . . . . . maritime pre-positioned equipment and
supplies
MPF . . . . maritime pre-positioning force
MPSRON . . maritime pre-positioning ships squadron
MRT . . . . medical regulating team
MSC . . . . Military Sealift Command
MT . . . . motor transport
MTMC . . . . . Military Traffic Management Command
MWSG . . . . Marine wing support group
MWSS . . . . Marine wing support squadron

N

NATO . . . . North Atlantic Treaty Organization
NBC . . . . nuclear, biological, and chemical
NBG . . . . naval beach group
NSE . . . . Navy support element
NVG . . . . night vision goggles

O

OCU . . . . orderwire control unit
OIC . . . . officer in charge
OPCON . . . . operational control

P

PEI . . . . principal end item
PLGR . . . . precision lightweight global positioning
system (GPS) receiver
POD . . . . port of debarkation

POE . . . . .port of embarkation

POG . . . . port operations group

POL . . . . petroleum, oils, and lubricants

Q

QSTAG . . . . . quadripartite standardization agreement

R

ROLMS . . . . .Retail Ordnance Logistics
Management System (Army)

RW . . . . rotary wing

S

SASSY . . . . .Supported Activity Supply System

SLRP . . . . . .survey, liaison, and reconnaissance party

SMU . . . . SASSY management unit

SOP . . . . standing operating procedure

SP . . . . .shore party

STANAG . . . . . . standardization agreement (NATO)

T

TACLOG . . . . .tactical-logistical group

TALCE . . . . .tanker airlift control element

TAMCN . . . . .table of authorized materiel
control number

TCAIMS . . . Transportation Coordinator's Automated
Information for Movement System

T/E . . . . .table of equipment

T/O . . . . table of organization

tm . . . . .team

TPFDD . . . . .time-phased force deployment data

TSB . . . . Transportation Support Battalion

U

UMCC . . . . unit movement control center

USTRANSCOM . . . . . . .United States Transportation
Command

W

WPS . . . . Worldwide Port System

SECTION II. DEFINITIONS

A

advance party—A task organization formed by the MAGTF commander that consists of personnel designated to form the nucleus of the arrival and assembly organizations.

amphibious assault—(DOD) The principal type of amphibious operation that involves establishing a force on a hostile or potentially hostile shore. (JP 1-02)

amphibious assault bulk fuel system—The US. Navy system of flexible, buoyant hose used to effect ship-to-shore transfer of fuels. Five thousand feet of 6-inch hose connects amphibious shipping to shore-based fuel storage systems located at the high water mark. (MCRP 5-12C)

amphibious assault fuel system (AAFS)—The Marine Corps' primary fuel storage system used to support amphibious operations. (extract from MCRP 5-12C)

amphibious force—An amphibious task force and a landing force together with other forces that are trained, organized, and equipped for amphibious operations. (Proposed for inclusion in JP 1-02 by JP 3-02.)

amphibious planning—The process of planning for an amphibious operation, distinguished by the necessity for concurrent, parallel and detailed planning by all participating forces. (extract from JP 1-02)

amphibious task force (ATF)—A Navy task organization formed to conduct amphibious operations. The amphibious task force, together with the landing force and other forces, constitutes the amphibious force. (Proposed for inclusion in JP 1-02 by JP 3-02.)

arrival and assembly area (AAA)—An area designated by Commander, MPF in coordination with the unified commander and host nation for arrival, offload, and assembly of forces and MPE/S, and preparations for subsequent operations.

arrival and assembly operations element (AAOE)—An agency in each MAGTF element and the NSE which coordinates the logistics functions of the offload of MPE/S and the arrival and assembly of forces.

arrival and assembly operations group (AAOG)—A staff agency of the MAGTF, composed of personnel from the MAGTF and a liaison from the NSE, to control the arrival and assembly operations.

B

basic load—(DOD, NAT'O) The quantity of supplies required to be on hand within, and which can be moved by, a unit or formation. It is expressed according to the wartime organization of the unit or formation and maintained at the prescribed levels. (JP 1-02)

beach organization—In an amphibious operation, the planned arrangement of personnel and facilities to effect movement, supply, and evacuation across beaches and in the beach area for support of a landing force. (JP 1-02)

beach support area (BSA)—In amphibious operations, the area to the rear of a landing force or elements thereof, established and operated by shore party units, which contains the facilities for the unloading of troops and materiel and the support of the forces ashore; it includes facilities for the evacuation of wounded, enemy prisoners of war, and captured materiel. (JP 1-02)

beachhead—A designated area on a hostile or potentially hostile shore that, when seized and held, ensures the continuous landing of troops and materiel, and provides maneuver space requisite for subsequent projected operations ashore. (JP 1-02)

beachmaster—The naval officer in command of the beachmaster unit of the naval beach group. (JP 1-02)

beachmaster unit (BMU)—A commissioned naval unit of the naval beach group designed to provide to the shore party a naval component known as a beach party which is capable of supporting the amphibious landing of one division (reinforced). (JP 1-02)

C

CLZ support team—Provides logistic support to the landing force and terminal control of landing craft, air cushion. (extract from NWP 3)

combat cargo officer (CCO)—(DOD) An embarkation officer assigned to major amphibious ships or naval staffs, functioning primarily as an adviser to and representative of the naval commander in matters pertaining to embarkation and debarkation of troops and their supplies and equipment and to the management of landing force operational reserve material (LFORM).

commander, amphibious task force (CATF)—The Navy officer designated in the order initiating the amphibious operation as the commander of the amphibious task force. (Proposed for inclusion in JP 1-02 by JP 3-02.)

commander, landing force (CLF)—The officer designated in the order initiating the amphibious operation as the commander of the landing force. (Proposed for inclusion in JP 1-02 by JP 3-02.)

concept of logistic support—A verbal or graphic statement, in a broad outline, of how a commander intends to support and integrate with a concept of operations in an operation or campaign. (JP 1-02)

coordinating authority—A commander or individual assigned responsibility for coordinating specific functions or activities involving forces of two or more military departments or two or more forces of the same Service. The commander or individual has the authority to require consultation between the agencies involved, but does not have the authority to compel agreement. In the event that essential agreement cannot be obtained, the matter shall be referred to the appointing authority. (extract from JP 1-02)

D

debarkation—(DOD) The unloading of troops, equipment, or supplies from a ship or aircraft (JP 1-02).

E

embarkation—(DOD) The process of putting personnel and/or vehicles and their associated stores and equipment into ships and/or aircraft. (JP 1-02)

F

flight ferry—The movement by self-deployment of the aircraft of the ACE to the AAA.

fly-in echelon (FIE)—Airlifted forces and equipment of the MAGTF and NSE plus aircraft and personnel arriving in the flight ferry of the ACE.

G

general unloading period—In amphibious operations, that part of the ship-to-shore movement in which unloading is primarily logistic in character, and emphasizes speed and volume of unloading operations. It encompasses the unloading of units and cargo from the ships as rapidly as facilities on the beach permit. It proceeds without regard to class, type, or priority of cargo, as permitted by cargo handling facilities ashore. (JP 1-02)

H

helicopter support team (HST)—A task organization formed and equipped for employment in a landing zone to facilitate the landing and movement of helicopterborne troops, equipment and supplies, and to evacuate selected casualties and enemy prisoners of war. (Joint Pub 1-02). It may be built around a nucleus of shore party and helicopter landing zone control personnel. (JP 3-02)

hydrography—(DOD, NATO) The science which deals with the measurements and description of the physical features of the oceans, seas, lakes, rivers, and their adjoining coastal areas, with particular reference to their use for navigational purposes. (JP 1-02)

I

initial unloading period—In amphibious operations, that part of the ship-to-shore movement in which unloading is primarily tactical in character and must be instantly responsive to landing force requirements. All elements intended to land during this period are serialized. (JP 1-02)

L

landing beach—(DOD, NATO) That portion of a shoreline usually required for the landing of a battalion landing team. However, it may also be that portion of a shoreline constituting a tactical locality (such as the shore of a bay) over which a force larger or smaller than a battalion landing team may be landed. (JP 1-02)

landing craft—(DOD, NATO) A craft employed in amphibious operations, specifically designed for carrying troops and equipment and for beaching, unloading, and retracting. Also used for logistic cargo resupply operations. (JP 1-02)

landing force (LF)—A Marine Corps or Army task organization formed to conduct amphibious operations. The landing force, together with the amphibious task force and other forces, constitute the amphibious force. (Proposed for inclusion in JP 1-02 by JP 3-02.)

landing schedule—(DOD) In an amphibious operation, a schedule which shows the beach, hour, and priorities of landing of assault units, and which coordinates the movements of landing craft from the transports to the beach in order to execute the scheme of maneuver ashore. (JP 1-02)

landing zone (LZ)—(DOD, NATO) Any specified zone used for the landing of aircraft. (JP 1-02)

landing zone control party—(DOD, NATO) Personnel specially trained and equipped to establish and operate communications devices from the ground for traffic control of aircraft/helicopters for a specific landing zone. (JP 1-02)

M

marine air-ground task force (MAGTF)—The Marine Corps principal organization for all missions across the range of military operations, composed of forces task-organized under a single commander capable of responding rapidly to a contingency anywhere in the world. The types of forces in the MAGTF are functionally grouped into four core elements: a command element, an aviation combat element, a ground combat element, and a combat service support element. The four core elements are categories of forces, not formal commands. The basic structure of the MAGTF never varies, though the number, size, and type of Marine Corps units comprising each of its four elements will always be mission dependent. The flexibility of the organizational structure allows for one or more

subordinate MAGTFs, other Service and/or foreign military forces, to be assigned or attached.

maritime pre-positioned equipment and supplies (MPE/S)—Unit equipment and sustaining supplies associated with a MAGTF and a NSE, which are deployed on maritime pre-positioning ships.

maritime pre-positioning force (MPF)—A task organization of units under one commander formed for the purpose of introducing a MAGTF and its associated equipment and supplies into a secure area The MPF is composed of a command element, a maritime pre-positioning ships (MPS) squadron, a MAGTF, and a Navy support element. (MCRP 5-12C)

maritime pre-positioning ships (MPS)—(DOD) Civilian-crewed, Military Sealift Command-chartered ships that are organized into three squadrons and are usually forward-deployed. These ships are loaded with pre-positioned equipment and 30 days of supplies to support three Marine expeditionary brigades. (JP 1-02)

maritime pre-positioning ships squadron (MPSRON)—A group of civilian-owned and civilian-crewed ships chartered by Military Sealift Command loaded with pre-positioned equipment and 30 days of supplies to support a MAGTF up to MEB size.

marshalling area—In amphibious operations, the designated area in which, as part of the mounting process, units are reorganized for embarkation; vehicles and equipment are prepared to move directly to embarkation areas; and housekeeping facilities are provided for troops by other units. (MCRP 5-12C)

N

naval beach group (NBG)—(DOD, NATO) A permanently organized naval command, within an amphibious force, comprised of a commander, and staff, a beachmaster unit, an amphibious construction battalion, and an assault craft unit, designed to provide an administrative group from which required naval tactical components may be made available to the attack force commander and to the amphibious landing force commander to support the landing of one division (reinforced). (JP 1-02)

naval beach unit—See naval beach group.

Navy cargo handling and port group (NAVCHAPGRU)—(DOD) The active duty, cargo handling battalion-sized unit composed solely of active duty personnel. (JP 1-02) These units are part of the operating forces and represent the Navy's capability for open ocean cargo handling.

Navy support element (NSE)—The maritime pre-positioning force element that is composed of naval beach group staff and subordinate unit personnel, a detachment of Navy cargo handling force personnel, and other Navy components, as required. It is tasked with conducting the off-load and ship-to-shore movement of maritime pre-positioned equipment/supplies. (JP 1-02)

nonscheduled waves—Units of the landing force held in readiness for landing during the initial unloading period but not included in scheduled or on-call waves.

O

offload preparation party (OPP)—A task organization of Navy and Marine maintenance, embarkation and cargo handling personnel deployed to the MPSRON before or during its transit to the objective area to prepare the ship's offload systems and embarked equipment for offload.

S

serial—An element or a group of elements within a series which is given a numerical or alphabetical designation for convenience in planning, scheduling, and control. (JP 1-02)

ship-to-shore movement—(DOD, NATO) That portion of the assault phase of an amphibious operation which includes the deployment of the landing force from the assault shipping to designated landing areas. (JP 1-02)

shore party—A task organization of the landing force, formed for the purpose of facilitating the landing and movement off the beaches of troops, equipment, and supplies; for the evacuation from the beaches of casualties and enemy prisoners of war; and for facilitating the beaching, retraction, and salvaging of landing ships and craft. It comprises elements of both the naval and landing forces. (JP 1-02)

survey, liaison, and reconnaissance party (SLRP)—A task organization formed from the MAGTF and NSE, which is introduced into the objective area prior to the arrival of the main body of the FIE to conduct initial reconnaissance, establish liaison with in-theater authorities, and initiate preparations for the arrival of the main body of the FIE and the MPSRON.

T

TACLOG group—Representatives designated by troop commanders to assist Navy control officers aboard control ships in the ship-to-shore movement of troops, equipment, and supplies. (JP 1-02)

tactical airfield fuel dispensing system (TAFDS)—An expeditionary system providing bulk fuel storage and dispensing facilities at airfields not having permanently installed fuel systems; also used to support fuel dispensing at established airfields. (MCRP 5-12C)

throughput—(DOD) In logistics, the flow of sustainability assets in support of military operations, at all levels of war, from point of origin to point of use. It involves the movement of personnel and materiel over lines of communications using established pipelines and distribution systems. (MCRP 5-12C)

Appendix G. References and Related Publications

Department of Defense Directive (DODD)

4500.9	Transportation and Traffic Management

Allied Tactical Publications (ATPs)

8(A)	Doctrine for Amphibious Operations
35(B)	Land Force Tactical Doctrine
36(A)	Amphibious Operations Ship to Shore Movement
39(A)	Amphibious Embarkation
46(A)	Air Drop Systems for Personnel and Supply Equipment

Joint Publications (JPs)

1-02	Department of Defense Dictionary of Military and Associated Terms
3-02	Joint Doctrine for Amphibious Operations
3-02.1	Joint Doctrine for Landing Force Operations
3-02.2	Joint Doctrine for Amphibious Embarkation
4-0	Doctrine for Logistic Support of Joint Operations
4-01	Joint Doctrine for the Defense Transportation System
4-01.3	JTTP for Movement Control
4-01.5	Joint Tactics, Techniques, and Procedures for Water Terminal Operations
4-01.6	Joint Tactics, Techniques, and Procedures for Joint Logistics over the Shore
4-01.7	Joint Tactics, Techniques, and Procedures for Use of Intermodal Containers in Joint Operations

Navy Supplement Publication (NAVSUP PUB)

505	Preparation of Hazardous Material for Military Air Shipment

Marine Corps Warfighting Publications (MCWPs)

2-1	Intelligence Operations
3-17	Engineer Operations
4-1	Logistics Operations
4-11	Tactical Level Logistics
4-11.1	Health Service Support Operations
4-11.5	Seabee Operations in MAGTF
6-22	Communications and Information Systems

Marine Corps Reference Publications (MCRPs)

4-11.3B	Movement of Units in Air Force Aircraft
4-11.3E	Multiservice Helicopter Sling-Load Volumes I, Basic Operations and Equipment, Volume II Single Point Rigging Procedures, Volume III Dual-Point Load Rigging Procedures
4-11.3F	Convoy Operations Handbook
5-12C	Marine Corps Supplement to the Department of Defense Dictionary of Military and Associated Terms

Marine Corps Orders (MCOs)

P4030.19	Preparing Hazardous Materials for Military Air Shipments
8010.1E	Class V(W) Planning Factors for Fleet Marine Force Combat Operations

Fleet Marine Force Manuals (FMFMs)

1-8/NWP 22-3	Ship-to-Shore Movement (under revision as MCWP 3-31.5)
4-2	The Naval Beach Group
4-6	Movements of Units in Air Force Aircraft (under revision as MCRP 4-12A)
47-47	Airdrop of Supplies and Equipment: Rigging Containers

10-553   Airdrop of Supplies and Equipment:
                                Rigging Ammunition

Army Technical Manual (TM)

38.50   Packaging, Materials Handling, and Preparing of
                                Hazardous Materials for Military Air Shipment

Army Field Manual (FM)

55-17   Terminal Operations Coordinator's Handbook

Army Technical Bulletin (TB)

55-46-1   Standard Characteristics (dimensions, weight, and
                                cube) for Transportability of Military Vehicles and
                                Other Outside/Overweight Equipment